Ladies DAY

ONE WOMAN'S GUIDE TO PRO BASEBALL

*To Rivka,
Thanks for all your support over the years!
Love
Cathy*

Ladies DAY

ONE WOMAN'S GUIDE TO PRO BASEBALL

Catherine
Rondina
&
Joseph
Romain

W
Warwick Publishing

© 1997 Joseph Romain and Catherine Rondina

All rights reserved. No part of this publication may be reproduced, stored in a retrieval system or data base, or transmitted in any form or by any means, electronic, mechanical, photocopying, recording, or otherwise, without prior permission of the publisher.

ISBN: 1-895629-80-2

Published by:
Warwick Publishing Inc., 24 Mercer Street, Toronto, Ontario M5V 1H3
Warwick Publishing Inc., 1424 N. Highland Avenue, Los Angeles, CA 90027

Distributed by:
Firefly Books Ltd., 3680 Victoria Park Avenue, Willowdale, Ontario M2H 3K1

Design: Diane Farenick
Photo Credits: The images in this book come from two sources. Chuck Cotchman of System Four Photography, Toronto, supplied all of the images of modern era players and fans; Ron McCulloch, baseball historian and writer, supplied all of the images of players from baseball's past, courtesy of his relationship with the National Baseball Hall of Fame, in Cooperstown.

Printed in Canada

The authors would like to thank the following people for their insights, encouragements, and reading of draft versions of the book. Thanks to Gail Ferguson, Zoey Adams, J.J. Duplacey, Hazel Ferguson, George Rondina, June Callwood and my BF's.

They would also like to extend their thanks to their publishers, Nick Pitt and Jim Williamson, and to the enthusiastic and capable crew at Warwick press, Diane Farenick, Kimberley Davison and Harry Endrulat.

This book is dedicated to: Hazel May Ferguson, who's home run over the third base line brought home three runs and the Dominion Ladies Baseball Championship of 1929, and Cathy's father, George Currie, who never missed a game, major league or little league, our Babe: her mother Rita "Babyface" Currie, her family, and especially her home team, George, Matthew and Nella.

INTRODUCTION

In 1883, Ladies Day was introduced as a promotion to encourage American women to come out to the park, free of charge, to look in on the game that had stolen the hearts of their menfolk. The idea was that by giving them a free look-see, women would come back with their purses opened, ready to pay for the privilege of watching the great American spectacle. It was a great success, and by the 1920s women made up such a huge proportion of the crowd, nobody would dare give away what they could sell for full price! We wish we could give this book away, but in the '90s, nothing is free.

Ladies Day: The Women's Guide to Pro Baseball is a book for women who don't believe that baseball is a man's world. It is a book for baseball fans, baseball widows, and those of you who want to know what all the fuss is about. The authors thought is was important that there be something available that would provide the basic information, painlessly, to the novice. So if you don't know anything about baseball, take heart and read on. By this time next week you'll know everything you need to have a good time at the ballpark. If you are already a fan, someone who already has a good time at the ballpark, you will find this compendium of oddities and curiosities an amusing diversion in the off-season.

The book has four parts: a glossary and who's who, a collection of curious facts, a set of great photographs from now and then, and some highlights of women's participation on the diamond.

Our glossary isn't exactly your standard dictionary. People don't exactly go around reading the dictionary for entertainment, and we wanted you to read this one, so we made it different: painless, informative, and, we hope, amusing. Most of the important baseball lingo, from Annie Oakley to Yogi Berraisms, is looked at in a way we hope will entertain and inform any reader — male, female, or otherwise. Feel free to dip in and out of the book. Though there may be some sense in starting at the beginning and working your way through, it isn't necessary. Part of the important language of baseball are player's names, so we have included some of the who's who from across history. You will find yesterday's legends and losers along with today's hottest hitters and handsomest hunks represented in the glossary. We hope you approve.

The photographs throughout this book come from some of the best shutterbugs in the game. They cover baseball from its earliest days right through to last season, and they should give you a pretty good idea of what to expect at the ballpark. They say that a picture is worth a thousand words. If that is true, our publisher owes us a lot of money.

Did you know that Marg Schott was not the first woman to control a major-league baseball team? No? Then did you know that a kid from the Midwest struck out the two greatest batters in the history of the game? No? Well, then, do you know the name of the game's first transsexual switch-hitter? No? Than you better pay attention to the sidebars. We believe this to be a prime selection of the sort of trivia that is worth gold at postgame gatherings. If you want to stump your chump, check out the compendium of odd and memorable facts that meander throughout the pages.

And last, but not least, is a curious history of women's participation in the game. A lot of men think baseball is an exclusively male domain. Well we're here to say that it just ain't so. Women have always been a big part of the game, and it hasn't always been playing softball on Sundays. It was never our intention to provide a thorough history of women's baseball, but you will find that our collection of Diamond Girls highlights some of the greatest players in the game.

In sum, *Ladies Day: The Women's Guide to Pro Baseball* is a compendium of baseball fact, fiction, and fun. If you read this book from cover to cover, you should know enough about the finer points of the game to really enjoy it, as well as knowing enough of the inside information to make you look like a dedicated fan.

THE A-Z OF BASEBALL

AARON, HANK: If you picked up this book because you want to know something about baseball, Hank Aaron is a good place to start. And that's convenient since there are no aardvarks playing in the major leagues. So we'll start there. Hank Aaron is the answer when the question is "Who hit more home runs than anybody else in baseball?" (How many? Hank Aaron hit 755.)

ABOARD: This is what every batter is trying to get. If he's going to ride home, he'd better get aboard before the whistle blows three times. There are many ways of saying that there are men on base, and "aboard" is a favorite among radio announcers. "Barry Bonds will come to bat with two aboard" is just a colorful way of telling us that there are two men on base for the next batter. Good Grief.

ACE: So what did you think it meant? A loser? The ace is a pitcher. He's expected to be a successful pitcher. That's why they call him an ace. But let's talk about it in September, OK? The difference between an ace in April, at the start of the season, and an ace in September is that there are more of them in April than there are in September.

ACTION PITCHER: An action pitcher really wants you to go for it. He often hasn't really got what it takes to be an ace, but he covers his shortcomings with teasers and good one-liners. The best thing about an action pitcher is that if you wait it out, he'll give you a pitch you can drive downtown. The action is sliders, curves, change-ups, forkballs. If an action pitcher hasn't got a fastball worthy of the name, they call him a junk man.

DID YOU KNOW?

That standout minor-league pitcher Jackie Mitchell struck out Babe Ruth and Lou Gerhig back to back in an exhibition game on May 11, 1931? The payoff? Baseball commissioner Kenesaw Mountain Landis canceled her minor-league contract the next day. He ruled that baseball was too demanding for women!

ADDING AND SUBTRACTING: The mathematics of pitchers' contract negotiations has become so convoluted that even the agents have to hire lawyers. Calculating the value of a pitcher involves arcane and bizarre formulas, which takes into account the ERA, wins, losses, balls, strikes, number of batters faced, all-star selections, subsidiary endorsement rights, and number of days between clean shirts. Pitchers and catchers, on the other hand, don't need to be mathematical whiz kids. But they have to be able to add and subtract. When the pitcher "adds one" or "subtracts one" from the signal he's been given, his catcher had better be up on his arithmetic. Say the catcher signals with two fingers, calling for, say, the curve ball, and the pitcher signals back that he wants to "add one." The pitcher is telling the catcher that he's going to throw the number three pitch; say, the forkball. So the catcher had better be able to add, or he's liable to get a swooping fastball upside the head.

ALIBI IKE: You know this guy. We all know this guy. Whatever went wrong, it wasn't his fault. The grass was lumpy, the sun was too bright, the lady in the second row distracted him. In kindergarten we called him a crybaby. Ball players feel the same about him as we do. There's only one guy worse than Alibi Ike, and that's Daniel Webster. (See also Webster, Daniel.)

ALOMAR, ROBERTO: If it weren't for his temper, Alomar would be known as one of the greatest second basemen who ever played the game. Unfortunately for Alomar, his claim to fame may be that he nearly caused the 1996 World Series schedule to collapse. In a late season game, umpire

John Hershbeck called Alomar out on a ball which was closer to the dugout than it was to the strike zone. In the argument which ensued, Hershbeck said something about Robbie's mother and "army boots." In response, the hotheaded Puerto Rican player spit in the umpire's face. When asked about the spit and the subsequent ejection from the game, Robbie was far from apologetic: He blamed the bad call on the fact that the umpire had "family problems." The five-game suspension issued by the league was not good enough for the American League umpires, and they had to be forced back to the ballpark under a court injunction.

AMERICAN LEAGUE: Known as the junior circuit because it was formed 15 years after the National League. Since 1901 there have been two major leagues: the AL and the NL. In the American League, the pitcher can be excused from batting duties in favor of a designated hitter, while in the NL, the pitcher must bat or leave the game. Now I may not be a geography expert, but I thought Canada was still a separate country. However, the Toronto Blue Jays play in the American League, and the Montreal Expos plays in the National League. So what nation are they talking about here? America? Canada? Or the merry old land of Oz?

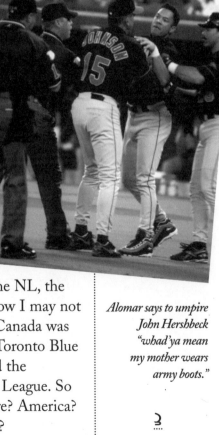

Alomar says to umpire John Hershbeck "whad'ya mean my mother wears army boots."

Brady Anderson gets Gail's vote for the best buns on the bench.

ANDERSON, BRADY: When Baltimore comes to the ballpark, look for Brady Anderson in center field. He hits, steals, and bunts with the best of them, and my friend Gail says he's got the best buns in Major League Baseball. (See also Rodriguez, Ivan.)

ANDERSON, SPARKY: In his one season with Philadelphia in 1959, George Lee Anderson hit .218. So why is he in this book? Well, for one thing, he has won more than 600 games in both leagues and has won 16 league championships; more than any other manager. In his first season as a manager, he won the National League Pennant with Cincinnati, where he won 5 divisional titles, 4 pennants, and 2 World Series Championships. Baseball isn't just about numbers, but with a guy like Sparky Anderson, it's important to know where he's been. When the Detroit Tigers finished a distant last in 1989, Sparky took some time off to reflect over his long career in baseball. "The great thing about baseball is when you're done, you'll only tell your grandchildren the good things. If they ask me about 1989, I'll tell them I had amnesia" He came back for spring training, but Sparky was never able to lead the Tigers out of the jungle again. Prior to his retirement he took the game in stride. "The only reason I'm comin' out here tomorrow is the schedule says I have to."

ANNIE OAKLEY: No relation to Baseball Annie. Annie Oakley is what a batter does when he has four balls. With four balls, it's no wonder they strut down the first baseline. (See also Base On Balls.)

APPEAL: Don't you hate this? You tell the guy he's out, and he gets down on his knees and starts begging for another chance. Umpires have no mercy for these guys. They waggle their thumbs and the guy slinks back to the dugout. I love it. But an appeal play is more complicated than you might think. If the defensive team thinks a batter "went around" or a runner missed a base, they have to appeal to the umpire who will decide whether or not the batter swung or the runner tagged. If the defensive team does not appeal, the ump will not give his opinion one way or the other.

AROUND THE HORN: Going around the horn means that the ball is hit to the left side of the infield and the third baseman scoops it up, throws to second, and the second baseman (or shortstop) throws to first for a double play. It's what they call a 5-4-3 double play. What does that mean? Get used to it, the fine points of baseball are more cryptic than Eastern religious rituals. The field positions all have numbers from one to nine. The pitcher is player number 1, the catcher is 2, the first baseman is 3, the second baseman is 4, the third baseman is 5, the shortstop is 6, the left, center, and right fielders are 7, 8, and 9 respectively. Got all that? Baseball is full of strange folklore, and you might as well know some of it. The most famous "around the horn" combination was a trio of fielders named Tinkers, Evers, and Chance.

ARTIFICIAL TURF: This stuff is worth its weight in gold. You never have to cut it, edge it, seed it, or argue with anybody about whose job all these things are. Given the choice between a gardener and artificial turf, I'm not sure which I'd choose. I like to think I'm environmentally sensitive, but considering the advantages of artificial turf, I'm not sure that nature has got the edge here. AKA: Astroturf

ASSIST: Baseball is a team sport. If the guys aren't cooperating, they're not going to be successful. A player who helps get a batter or runner out will be credited with an assist. For example, if the ball is hit sharply to the shortstop who grabs it and throws to first before the batter gets there, the shortstop will be credited with an assist. Does anybody care about this sort of statistic? Yes and no. If you are an agent, you count everything a player does and put a price tag on it. The number of assists your man gets in the season might be worth

Diamonds are a girls BEST FRIEND

Baseball, America's National Pastime, has roots which stretch across the Atlantic Ocean to Great Britain. In England, countless generations of women and girls have passed their time playing a stick-and-ball game called 'rounders'. Their husbands and sons were on the village green playing 'cricket', a bat and ball game which is played on a 'pitch', divided into 'innings', and supervised by an 'umpire'. So all this time we've been led to believe that mum was in the kitchen making apple crumble, when actually she was hitting line drives and sliding into second base. And it's not as if she stopped playing when mum, and her game, moved Stateside and developed an American flair. In America, women still don't play Big League baseball - we're not allowed to, no matter how good we are - but that hasn't kept us from playing our own game. From the days of the Bloomer Girls to the 1996 Olympics, women have hit and run with the best of them. We don't play Big League ball, but that doesn't mean it's not our game. Since the time that Alexander Cartwright and the New York Knickerbockers were challenging all comers, women have followed the game with gusto, and supplied all the snacks. Follow the 'diamonds' for some of the highlights of women on the field.

a few bucks if the number is high. Otherwise, not too many of us pay attention to the number of assists a player gets.

AT-BAT: The guy with the long stick over his shoulders is at bat. But what he does with it determines whether or not they call it an "official" at-bat. If he walks, is hit by the pitch, sacrifices, or does almost anything except get a hit or make an out, then being at bat doesn't count as an at-bat. Get it? Well, when you get to the end of this book, you will. Hang in there. AKA: AB

BACKSTOP: The backstop is a fine screen or fence behind home plate. It is designed to keep any foul tips, passed balls, or wild pitches from making their way into the crowd of fans who paid big bucks for the best seats. The catcher is also referred to as the backstop. If he does his job as well as the fence, he's probably going to make the Hall of Fame. And if he's *the* Bench, he's already made the Hall of Fame. (See also Bench, Johnny; Catcher.)

BAG: There are three of them. You can step on them, slide into them, steal them, touch them, trip over them, and hug them. But these bags won't hold anything. At the risk of sounding like the male anatomy unit in a grade 11 health class, we might also point out that it is called a sack. Everything that is said about the bag is true of the sack. (See also Base.)

BAGWELL, JEFF: What Jeff bags best is home runs. And it's no wonder. The guy has arms like Popeye! Bagwell is a franchise player in Houston, where he plays first base. Keep an eye on this MVP winner to set records over the next few seasons.

BAIL OUT: When these guys bail out, it's not because they broke the law. It's self-defense. If somebody threw a ball at your head at about a hundred miles an hour, you'd do the same thing. Bail out. (See also Duster.)

BALK: A balk is as difficult to observe as it is to figure out where they got the word from. The only thing we could think of was it sounds like what a deranged chicken says. But why would the chicken say "balk" whenever the pitcher did something wrong? How would the chicken know? Next question! Normally, a balk is only called when there is one or more runners on base. When the umpire calls a balk, the runners advance one base, but the batter does not. (There are exceptions to this: See also Walk.) A balk is called when (a) the pitcher does not come to a set position; (b) the pitcher does not throw to the plate after making a motion in that direction; (c) the pitcher pretends to throw home or to a base; (d) the pitcher throws to home plate or to a base without first stepping in the direction of the throw; (e) the pitcher pretends to have the ball and stands on or near the pitcher's rubber; (f) the pitcher throws the ball when the catcher is out of position (the catcher must be in the catcher's box); (g) the pitcher pumps his arm more than twice before letting the pitch go; and (h) the pitcher makes any illegal pitch. Still with me? This game has more rules about what you can do with your hands and lips than a chaperone at the senior sock hop.

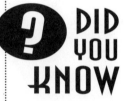

That Sherry Davis began her job as the first full-time female public address announcer in major league baseball on April 12, 1993, at Candlestick Park? They say women like to talk; well, when Davis talks, 30,000 people listen!

DID YOU KNOW?

That Geri Lisa Fitz, top notch hopeful with the Colorado Silver Bullets women's baseball club, began her professional career as Mr. Gerald Fitz, *shortstop for the (all male) Kentucky Bourbons ball club? Fitz may be baseball's only transsexual slugger.*

BALL HAWK: Baseball has its share of birdbrains. The ball hawk is a rare bird of prey who lives in the outfield. No matter where the ball is hit, the ball hawk can be seen swooping across the grass to snatch it out of the air. Their natural habitat is deep in center field, but the fastest ones might be sighted as far south as second base.

BALTIMORE CHOP: Take one fastball, a very spicy one, if you can get it, pound it on top with a baseball bat, and smoke it in front of home plate. The secret to serving a perfect Baltimore chop is to make it *soufflé*, that is, to make it rise up so high that by the time it comes down, it's too late for the batter to be thrown out at first. AKA: Chopper, butcher boy, bounder, topper

BASE: The bases are the three white squares in the infield. They are 90 feet from home plate and from each other. They are sort of the point of the game. Getting from one to the other is the object of baserunning; if you want to get home, you have to touch all three bases before you get there. (See also Bag.)

BASE HIT: Next to "outs," base hits are what you're going to see most at the ballpark. And that's good, because base hits are exciting, once you know what to watch for. (See also Getting to First Base.)

BASE ON BALLS: This has nothing directly to do with getting to base on the strength of male hormones. But it is about having the balls to wait for your pitch. A batter who has the stamina to resist swinging at four pitches which are out of the zone will "Annie Oakley" to first base on balls. (See also Annie Oakley; Walk.) AKA: BB

10

Ladies DAY

BASE RUNNER: A runner is any player who gets to first base. He can get there by any of seven methods (See Getting to First Base), including walking, but they still call him a base runner. Why would they call a guy a runner when he's walking? This makes as much sense as calling a guy a hitter when he strikes out. But who ever said baseball lingo made sense? If it did, we would'nt need "A-Z."

BASEBALL ANNIE: This is about the least offensive name for the women who hang around the ballpark after the game. She's not looking for autographs, though she is collecting players. But the stats she's interested in have little to do with on-field performances. Got the picture? You can find her name and number scratched in little black books and in the clubhouse backhouse.
AKA: Groupie

BASELINE: To understand baseball, you have to understand that it is obsessed with tradition. They may tinker with the fine points of the game, but even allowing players to wear facial hair nearly caused a revolution! The baselines

Rickey Henderson, some say the greatest base runner in history. Certainly one heck of a base thief.

11
A-Z

Diamonds are a girl's BEST FRIEND

DOTTIE KAMENSEK

When baseball needed somebody to salvage it from the player drought caused by World War II, they called on women to do the job. Philip K Wrigley, of Chicago Cubs and chewing gum fame, organized a league of professional women softball players known as the All American Girls Base Ball League. Dottie Kamensek, first baseman for the Rockford Peaches, was simply the best player in the league. Wally Pipp, former fist-baseman for the New York Yankees called her the "fanciest-fielding first baseman I've ever seen, man or woman…". When the league chose positions for the All Star team, they gave Kamensek the nod, and for the rest of her professional career, she remained the All Star first baseman. And Dottie could wallop the ball, too! The AAGBL's batting champion for 1946 and 47 established one of the most remarkable batting records in any books. In nearly 4,000 times at bat, she struck out only 81 times.

have been the same since Alexander Cartright first paced them out in 1845; they don't go up and down every season like that other American preoccupation, the hemline. The baselines extend from home plate at 90 degrees, passing first and third base at 90 feet and meeting the home run fence about 200 feet later.

BASES LOADED: You don't have to fill up the bases with tequila to get them loaded. You have to fill them up with such things as frozen ropes, Texas leaguers, and Baltimore chops. In any case, you have to put strong, handsome young men on all three bases and have less than three "outs." Got it? The only way a batter can get a grand slam is to have the bases loaded.

BASKET CATCH: We haven't shifted sports here, this is still baseball. When a player catches a fly ball with his glove held in front of him, below the belt, and above the knees, it's called a basket catch. A Gardener will often use a basket to catch a can of corn. We're not making this stuff up! (See also Can of Corn.)

BAT AROUND INNING: This sounds like you've had a few too many cups of foam, and you're buying a round of bats, but it's not. The bat around inning is when all the players get a turn at bat before three outs are made. It usually means a lot of runs have scored. It also usually means that the team who has one will win the game.

BAT BOY: He doesn't wear a cape and mask and fight little criminals, though he does wear a uniform and deal with unsavory characters. The bat boy is the kid who looks after the equipment in the

> **? DID YOU KNOW**
>
> *That night games began in 1935 when Cincinnati's Crosley Field installed lights around the ballpark? I bet a lot of ball players were playing night games long before anybody turned on the lights.*

dugout. You can see him scuttling around the backfield handing new balls to the umpire or handing out the bats.

BATTER'S BOX: I've seen some batters that I'd like to pack up and ship to my cousin Rita in Des Moines, but I've never found a carton big enough. What I didn't know was that they already designed one! In fact they make them for right-handed and left-handed batters! The batter's box is that rectangle marked out around home plate. The batter must stand in the batter's box when the pitcher throws the ball. I've seen some batters that look so good I'd like to pack them up and ship'em to Rita. I wonder how much postage I'd need to get Joe Carter to Iowa?

BATTERY: This isn't the sort of battery that you get a charge out of, though it better have a lot of spark. The battery is like an eatery; you eat in an eatery, and you bat in a battery. It's what they call a pitcher and catcher.

BATTING AVERAGE: A batter's average is always more important than an average batter, though even an average batter has a batting average, just not a very good one. Which is why he is an average batter at best. In fact at first glance, there isn't much difference between an average batter's batting average and a better batter's average. Got all that? It's simple: In baseball, a guy who averages four hits every 10 times at bat is an unbelievably successful hitter. They would call him a four hundred (.400) hitter. If he's still batting .400 in August, they would call him "The Next Ted Williams." A .320 hitter is a player who is having a very good year. The closer to .350 he gets, the fatter his bonus options on his contract get. If your

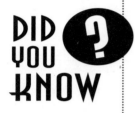

DID YOU KNOW?

That the New York Yankees have won the World Series more times than any other ball club? The Yanks have captured 21 world titles since their first win in 1923.

team has more than a couple of players who are .300 hitters, then they are probably contenders for the championship. A .200 hitter is either a pitcher, is sweating out a slump, or does not have to negotiate his contract this year. If you have more than a couple of .200 hitters in your lineup, the general manager may be looking for work. (See also Stengle, Casey; Williams, Ted.)

BATTING HELMET: You think you need a lot of accessories? These guys have got designer accessories for every occasion. When they come to bat, you will see them sporting klunky bonnets with their number on the back. There are two fundamental things wrong with the batting helmets, however. In the first place, they look ridiculous. In the second place, why do they call them batting helmets when they all wear them for running the bases?

BEAN BALL: Talk about your poor sports! A bean ball is a blemish on the game. When a pitcher throws a bean ball, he's throwing the ball at a batter's head. It's ugly, cowardly, and has no business in the game.

BEAR DOWN: What could a man possibly know about bearing down? You want to talk about pain? I'll tell you about pain. Ball players might do some amazing things, but there are

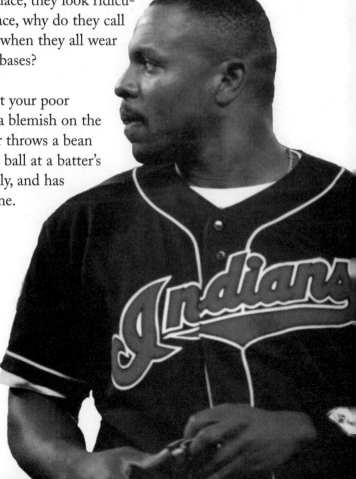

Albert "Ding-Dong" Belle.

limits to the wonders men can achieve. When a pitcher bears down, he's not lying on a table with his feet in the stirrups, he's just throwing the ball harder.

BELLE, ALBERT: This hotheaded Cleveland outfielder is what they call a loose cannon. And they're not just talking about his throwing arm. Often called "the best player in baseball," Belle has been known to throw temper tantrums on and off the field. In fact a *Sports Illustrated* photographer who had the nerve to snap a shot of Belle on field was thanked with a strike thrown right into his telephoto lens.

Albert "who said I was crazy?" Belle.

BENCH, JOHNNY: When they call somebody a "bench player," they don't mean the guy is like Johnny Bench, though that would be very high praise. Bench joined the Cincinnati Reds in 1967 and took the National League's Rookie of the Year honors —the first catcher to ever win that title. Bench was a fantastic defensive player, winning more golden gloves than he had fingers. But he was quite a fellow with the bat as well, winning the home run derby twice and the RBI contest three times. Bench was selected for the all-star team every year from 1968-77 and was still good enough to play all-star ball in 1983, his last year in the game. So when a team is said to have bench strength, they only wish they had a bunch of guys like Johnny sitting on it.

BENCH STRENGTH: With 20 guys weighing in at nearly 200 pounds and each sitting on a bench, it better be pretty solid. But that's not exactly what the expression refers to, though it's close. On most ball clubs, there is an elite group who have everyday field assignments and a smaller group who only get to play when one of the regulars is out of the lineup for some reason or other. These extra guys are your bench. Can they hit? Can they field? Can they run bases? Can they throw a ball 300 feet and hit the catcher's glove? The real and potential performance of these "utility players" is what is known as bench strength. If you want to play baseball in October, you need more than down-filled warm-up jackets: You'd better have a strong bench.

BICHETTE, DANTE: Bichette has been raising fire and brimstone around the National League lately, so he's somebody you might want to look out for. The infernal Floridian hit 40 homers and brought in 128 runs in 1995, tops in the Senior Circuit in every department, including the fire department.

A baseball. Also known as a "pill," "pea," "pellet," "apple," "horsehide," or "tomatoe."

? DID YOU KNOW

That in the 1927 season, Babe Ruth hit 60 home runs and his Yankee teammate Lou Gerhig hit 47 home runs? Their 107 homers that season led fans to dub this lineup in the batting order "Murderers Row."

Diamonds are a girls BEST FRIEND

JOANNE WINTER

When the girls of Summer played in the All American Girls Baseball League, they all trembled in anticipation of Winter. Joanne Winter. She signed up with the Racine Belles as a starting pitcher for 75 dollars a week, and finished the season with a respectable 11 wins and 11 losses, but she led her team to the league championship and the 'World Series' of women's baseball. The next few seasons saw Winter losing her grip on the game. Her underhand style of pitching was a dying art, and was quickly being replaced by the faster sidearm pitching seen around many of the league's ball parks. Winter adapted, learning a new style of underhand pitch that left the batters gawking. By 1946, Winter was once again the frosty contender of her rookie year, and went 33-10, striking out 183 batters, and recording a startling 63 consecutive shut-out innings. That record stands today, and earned her a spot in baseball history. You can see Winter's warm smile at the Baseball Hall of Fame in Cooperstown, New York.

BLACK SOX: The name has nothing to do with the White Sox's laundry detergent. But it does have something to do with dirty laundry. In 1919, eight members of the Chicago team were accused of fixing games for the Mob during the World Series. Shoeless Joe Jackson, a shoe-in for the Hall of Fame, was one of them. Jackson, who hit .375 for the series, never admitted to being part of the fix, but they banned him for life anyway. One of baseball's most enduring quotes comes from the courthouse steps after Jackson was found guilty. A kid called out as the players left the court: "Say it ain't so, Joe." (See also Jackson, Joe.)

BLEACHERS: No, this has nothing to do with BHD (Bad Hair Day) — although you might want to wear a hat to protect your head from sun stroke when you sit in the bleachers. This section, often referred to as the "cheap seats" is where you'll find the true fans. The loyal followers who risk nose bleeds and vertigo for even a bird's-eye-view of the ball game.

DID YOU KNOW

That the St. Louis Cardinals were controlled by a woman in 1916? Helen Britton inherited the team from her uncle and for the next five years ran the team's front office.

The Chicago White Sox, or was that Black Sox?

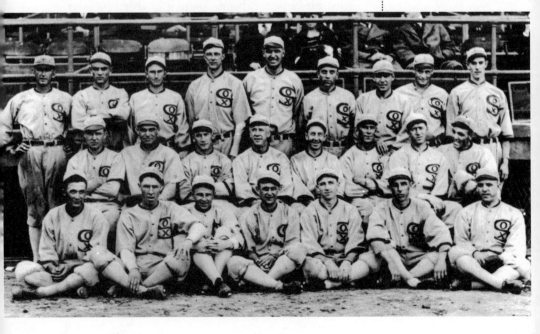

DID YOU KNOW

That in 1992, the World Series became truly international when it was played for the first time outside the United States in Canada? Canadians celebrated coast-to-coast when their Toronto Blue Jays won back-to-back World Championships in 1992 and 1993.

BLOCKING THE PLATE: Have you ever tried to carve up a turkey on Thanksgiving? Everybody is hungry and they're all hovering over you, dipping in for tasters. In my kitchen, when I block the plate, I use the carving knife. In baseball, they use the catcher. If the catcher doesn't do this well, he may keep all of his teeth, but he'll be using them to chomp hotdogs in minor-league ballparks. The catcher is expected, when some 200-pound galoot is steaming in from third base, to position himself between home plate and third base to await the ball. If the ball arrives before the runner, the catcher will tag him and try to hold on to the ball while he is sent sprawling behind home plate. The runner, of course, is trying to knock the ball free or the catcher silly. In the first case, he is home free, in the second, he gets some revenge. In the event that the fielders are not able to get the ball to the catcher before the runner arrives, the catcher will either try to slow the runner down with his body or get the hell out of the way!

BOGGS, WADE: Baseball is full of head cases, and Boggs is a league leader in eccentricity. The guy has batting numbers which are the envy of modern

20

Ladies DAY

Blocking the plate. The definition of dirty work.

baseball, so whatever weird rituals he performs, they must be doing something. Watch for the Hebrew letters he draws in the dirt at home plate and the unswerving path he wears into the grass on his way to and from the field. If you care to get up early, you could find him jogging every morning at exactly 7:17a.m. Now is that standard time or daylight savings?

BONDS, BARRY: If you get a chance to watch Barry Bonds play, get seats on the first-base side of the diamond. And bring binoculars. Watching Bonds bobbing and dodging at first base is definitely worth the price of a field-level ticket. He doesn't play first base — he just passes by on his way home. The binoculars are to get a better view of him after he steals second.

BOX SEATS: If you are ever invited to sit in the box seats, don't bring a box lunch. People with more money than they know what to do with sit there. They don't eat hotdogs. They eat veal sausages. They don't drink beer, they drink Perrier and lime. And they wear leisure suits and white loafers. On second thought, if you are ever invited to sit in the box seats, take a gracious rain check and enjoy the game with the real fans in the bleachers.

BREAKING BALLS: How do you break a man's spirit? Breaking balls. But not the way you might think. You throw him a curve, a slider, a forkball, or some other "breaking pitch." Balls that dipsy doodle on their way to the plate are called breaking balls.

BRUSH RULES: There are no known rules governing the brush the umpire uses to sweep off the plate. They don't care if he uses a Hoover! Brush Rules govern the number of umpires used in World Series Games. If your team makes it to the "Greatest Show On Earth," it'll be handy to know about the Brush Rules. Somebody will notice that there are umpires in the outfield, and *you* will know that under the Brush Rules of 1904, World Series Games have two extra umpires. They're named for a guy called John T. Brush who refused to put his American League team into the Series unless there were some changes to the rulebook.

Bona fide baseball wacko, Wade Boggs

BULL PEN: Maybe you thought this was where they all sat around shootin' the bull; but that's the clubhouse. The bull pen is where they keep the prime hunks. Each team has 25 men dressed for the game. About 15 of them are available to play infield and outfield positions, and they sit in the dugout. The other guys are pitchers, and they sit in the bull pen. The bull pen is a fenced in area located in foul territory, usually in the outfield, and is equipped with two pitcher's mounds, a dugout telephone, and closed-circuit television. But they're not watching soap operas out there; the only thing on television is the battery. They also call the men who sit there the bull pen. The bull pen is the group of pitchers who will be called upon to come into a game which is already in progress. You will find the long man, the middle reliever, the mop up man, the junk man, and the closer all sitting around eating sunflower seeds in the bull pen. When the starting pitcher is having trouble keeping the manager satisfied, they put in a phone call to the bull pen to get somebody up and warming. A guy or two will stand up and start throwing the ball. If that isn't enough to get the pitcher straightened out, the manager will walk out to the mound, take the ball away, and signal to the bull pen for a fresh pitcher. The guy that comes charging out of the bull pen when they open the gate will be full of spit and vinegar and will keep throwing until the manager tells him to stop. The starter is spent, so they put him out to pasture for a few days.

BURKE, KITTY: Kitty Burke is the only woman to ever bat in a major-league game. On July 31, 1935, Burke and her friends were part of an overflow crowd at the Cincinnati ballpark who were allowed to stand in the foul area along the baselines. When Babe Herman squeezed through the crowd to take his turn at bat, Burke grabbed the bat from his hands, and while her friends held Herman back, Kitty sauntered into the batter's box. The pitcher, Daffy Dean, shrugged and tossed the ball underhand. Burke smacked it down the first baseline and minced along to first, where Dean greeted her with the ball. She didn't make it to first base, but she made it into the history books.

? DID YOU KNOW

That in the early 1900s, Amanda Clement, the first woman umpire in organized ball, called the balls and strikes in the Nebraska League, in the Dakota's League, and in loops as long forgotten as the famed Iowa Baseball Confederacy. Amanda Clement was also recorded as having thrown a ball 275 feet. Today, she is regarded not only as a great player, but also as a "mother of the rulebook."

Diamonds are a girls BEST FRIEND

In the 1840's when a bunch of bankers and lawyers were refining 'rounders', the game women had been playing for centuries, their wives and daughters had more to worry about than whether or not the men allowed them to play the new game: they couldn't vote, divorce, or even attend college. In 1865 Vasser College opened it's doors to women, and before they reached their sophomore year, the girls had dividied themselves up into teams and joined the fun. I don't know how it could have been much fun playing baseball in high-button shoes and floor length skirts, but it was more fun than, say, sewing. But sewing is important, too, as we'll see later. In the 1870's women's games were popular entertainment. But it wasn't baseball; it was pre-game entertainment, like 19th Century Dallas Cowgirls. In frilly blouses and floor length skirts. Which is where the sewing comes in.. Fashion guru Amelia Bloomer sewed a line up the middle of a skirt, creating the fashion sensation of the season and liberating women ball players with one snip of the shears: Bloomer Girls. And the Bloomer Girls played real baseball.

BUNT: A bunt is a very small hit. It's not that the batter lacks the strength to hit the thing properly, he *wants* a very small hit. The idea is to hit the ball beyond the reach of the catcher, but not hard enough to reach the pitcher or a baseman. There are two good reasons for bunting: (a) Sometimes you will do anything to get to first base — like accepting "I have to visit my sick cousin tonight" as an excuse for canceling a date. Next Saturday night better mean dinner and flowers! (b) A heavy hitter will lay down a sacrifice bunt to move a teammate along from first to second, or second to third: It's like agreeing to date your best friend's cousin Ralph so that she and Hank the Hunk can get past first base. (See also Suicide Squeeze Play.)

BUSH LEAGUE: Everybody is running from something. You may be running from that home perm and those platform shoes from the 1970s. Ball players are running from the Bush Leagues. The minors. They have to ride buses and eat at Howard Johnsons. Nobody calls their cabs or pays their room service bills for them. On the other hand, if they boot a routine ground ball or give up six runs in the ninth, nobody really cares.

CAMINITI, KEN: My friend Julia came to the Dodgers game with me, and we sat in the front row across from third base. Julia went out to the snack bar in the seventh inning and came back just as Caminiti was chasing a high foul ball in front of us. He leaned over the wall, jabbed his glove into her nachos, and scooped the ball out with a gob of cheese whiz and catchup. Without missing a beat, Julia yelled over to him: "You want a soda with that cheeseball, Mac?" Caminiti was cool. He tossed her the ball.

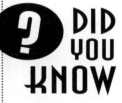

DID YOU KNOW

That first basemen wear mittens instead of gloves? The mitt was originally developed to protect the catcher's hand but migrated up the first baseline, where many of the balls thrown are coming in as fast as a pitched ball.

DID YOU KNOW?

That Pam Postema, the only woman among 100 candidates at umpire school, finished 17th out of 100 people and still had to put up with 13 years of abuse in the minors? She worked more than 2,000 games, and then baseball told her "Go away. No girls allowed." She filed and won a sexual discrimination suit in the U.S. Supreme Court, but the pain is so deep that she can't bear to watch a ball game.

CAN OF CORN: Men. They're obsessed with two things, and one of them is food. But my guess is that an outfielder would like to be served a can of corn any day! When the ball is hit high into the shallow outfield, the players say that it's like catchin' a can of corn falling off of a high shelf. A can of corn is an easy out. So what do they call it in the infield? Popcorn?

CANSECO, JOSE: This all-American slugger isn't exactly "all" American after all. He was born in Havana, Cuba, in 1964. There are a lot of records in baseball, but there are

Jose Canseco: an all-American slugger.

only a few that can't be broken and Canseco has one. He was the first player to hit 40 home runs and steal 40 bases in one season.

CARTER, JOE: Most people think of Joe Carter as the guy who hit a home run that knocked the World Series right out of the United States, but I think of him as the player most likely to smile in any situation. Joe has always been a streaky hitter, but at the end of the season, when they count up all the numbers, Carter's name is always near the top of the heap. No wonder he's always smiling!

One is the World Series Trophy, the other is the man who brought it to Canada, Joe Carter.

CARTWRIGHT, ALEXANDER JOY: This is the guy who really invented baseball. Cartwright and his friends, the Knickerbockers Base Ball Club, were mostly lawyers, stockbrokers, and merchants, which is probably why baseball players of today get paid so much money. I mean, the idea that baseball is a gentleman's game has gone the way of whalebone stays, but they still figure that they should be rich if they're gonna play professionally. Does this make sense to anybody out there? (See also Cooperstown; Doubleday, Abner.)

CATCHER: The guy squatting down behind home plate. No, not the umpire; the good-looking guy with the glove. There's more to being a catcher

The primary architect of baseball, Alexander Cartwright.

than successfully wrapping your glove around the balls that hitters don't hit. (See also Backstop; Tools of Ignorance.)

CATCHER INTERFERENCE: You wouldn't expect baseball players to cheat, would you? Well they steal don't they? They'll do anything to get an advantage. Watch the catcher when he's working. He's about as close to the batter as anybody could imagine, and it wouldn't take much for him to "tip" the bat as the swing comes around. If he does this successfully, the batter will probably miss the ball. If he gets caught, the batter gets a free pass to first base.

CELLAR: Last place. Nobody likes it in the cellar. It's dark, it's damp, and there's laundry piling up. To get out of the cellar usually means hitching up your breeches and working your way through your fears, your weak spots, and mountains of ironing.

CHANGE UP: It's like makeup: The whole idea is to use it without looking like you're using it. If you're wearing enough makeup to make Elizabeth Arden blush, then you've probably got something to hide. Like you've got a hide that needs hiding. The key to the change up is that it does not look like a change at all. A change up looks exactly like a fastball. The only difference between the two is that for the change up, the pitcher holds the ball loosely in his hand, resulting in a slower pitch, which the batter mistakes for a real fastball. The slower speed of the pitch is intended to confuse the batter who will be spinning on his heels before the ball reaches home. AKA: Changer, off speed pitch

DID YOU KNOW

That in 1928, the American Junior League formed a baseball association as "a means of teaching practical Americanism to the youth of the country"? Girls from across the country signed up for their lessons in Americanism, so a new rule was passed by the AJL: No girls allowed. American girls were stung by this lesson in Americanism for 50 years, when in the 1970s the ruling was found to contravene the Constitution and was unceremoniously reversed.

CHARITY HOP: When I heard there were charity hops in baseball, I was all set to put on my pleated skirt and bobbysocks. That was before I learned that a charity hop had nothing to do with dancing, or raising money for good causes. When a player gets a charity hop, it means the ball takes one more bounce than anybody expects, allowing the hitter to get to base before the fielder has time to throw him out. I'd still rather bop till I drop, but the only dancing these guys do is the chin music two step.

CHIN MUSIC: The dance macabre of baseball. Chin music is intended to charm the batter off the plate, but in the hands of a junk man, it might be the "Last Tango in Paris." If the pitcher thinks the batter is snuggling up a little too close and looking a little too comfortable, he might whistle up a little chin music to dance the guy back with a high hard one. For a good pitcher, it is known as a brush back; for a struggling pitcher, it might be known as a bean ball. (See also Bean Ball.)

CHOKE: The inability to perform under pressure. It's perfectly normal. Lots of guys have this problem. The only difference in baseball is that he can't try again in the morning.

CHOKE UP: Don't confuse this with choking. It has nothing to do with being unable to perform and everything to do with getting a grip on things. It's a matter of physics. If the bat is shorter, it goes around faster. Some batters will grip the bat a little higher up on the handle to get a little more speed. For reasons which defy explanation, they call it choking up.

CIRCUS PLAY: It's about what it sounds like. It's one of those embarrassing moments in the game when everybody looks like a clown. They juggle the ball, trip over their own two feet, crash into each other, and generally look like Bush Leaguers. A circus play can have a devastating effect on a team. Once these overweight egos start feeling stupid, it's hard to get back into the swing of things. They might be looking like champs before it happens, but after a circus play they look like *chimps* for the rest of the game. And to further confuse things, the term Circus Play is also used to describe an outstanding display of athletic prowess!

CLEANUP: The best hitter on the team cleans up. Right. In my house, the slowest eater cleans up. In baseball, the cleanup man *is* the best hitter. So why does he have to clean up? Not because the guys ahead of him have made a mess. Just the opposite. The cleanup hitter is the fourth guy in the batting order. Since he is the best hitter, the odds are that if there is anybody on base, he'll hit them home. They should use this line at my house. At least I'd feel better about washing the pots and pans.

CLOTHESLINE: With all the money in professional baseball, you'd think they would invest in a dryer! But in baseball, the clothesline is not something you peg your wet undies to; in fact you can't really peg *anything* to it. At the ballpark, a clothesline is a sharply hit line drive. Before anything can be pegged to it, you have to be sure that the far end of the line is not an outfielder with an outstretched glove.

? DID YOU KNOW

That in 1922, a minor-league first baseman named Lizzie Murphy played on an all-star team comprised of the best players from the American and New England Leagues? Six years later, she appeared as the National League all-star first baseman, thus becoming the first person to play for both an American and a National League all-star team!

CLUBHOUSE: Boys will always be boys. After they're done their chores, they all go to the clubhouse. They probably have secret handshakes too. The clubhouse is just what it was when we were kids. It's a special place where they have cold drinks and good stuff to eat, and nobody can go there without being a member of the club, or a special invited guest.

CLUTCH PLAYER: You know the guys who drive cars so low that you can't get in gracefully if you're wearing a skirt? They like to think of themselves as real men just because they have to use both feet to drive. Fortunately, their hands are busy shifting gears, too. It's not the same in baseball. Clutch players have busy hands, but they don't need all that chrome and fuzzy dice to make themselves look like real men. The team is down a couple of runs, there are two out, it's late in the game, some guy comes off the bench, and everybody knows he's gonna hit the ball. And he does. This is a clutch player. A guy who has what it takes to turn an opportunity into an achievement.

COMMISSIONER OF BASEBALL: Professional baseball is a private club. To join, you have to have more money than Fort Knox, you have to have a baseball team, and you have to agree to play by the rules. Having rules means you need somebody to enforce them. In baseball, that's the commissioner. The commissioner of baseball is like the umpire for owners. He governs all of Major League Baseball and makes big important decisions. When Jackie Mitchell, a young girl playing in the minor leagues, struck out Babe Ruth and Lou Gehrig back-to-back in an exhibition game, Judge Kenesaw

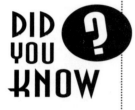

DID YOU KNOW

That baseball was played in Beachville, Ontario, in 1838? This is the year before Abner *Doubleday was supposed to have invented the game in Cooperstown, New York. Don't you wish these guys would get their story straight?*

Diamonds are a girls BEST FRIEND

MAUD NELSON

Baseball historians haven't' paid much attention to the women in the game until lately, so it's no surprise that Maud Nelson isn't exactly a household name. But she didn't do much to help herself avoid obscurity, either. Over the course of her life she went by the names Nelson, Neilson, Olson, Brida and Dellacqua. From the age of 16, Nelson was among the top female players of her day. In 1908, when the opportunities for women players were pretty limited, she organized her own team, the Cherokee Indian Base Ball Club. Three years later she bought the Western Bloomer Girls, and managed the squad's barnstorming tours. At the age of 41 most major leaguer pitchers are all washed up, but not Nelson - She was still pitching for the Boston Bloomer Girls. And even when she finished with the Boston Bloomers, she wasn't finished with baseball. In the early 1920's she and her husband, Constante Dellacqua bought a franchise and organized the All Star Ranger Girls. When she finally did retire, Nelson found a comfortable home - just a stone's throw from Wrigley Field.

DID YOU KNOW?

That television's first baseball game was aired in 1939 — 100 years after Abner Doubleday is said to have invented it? Nobody knows who might have played in 1839, but in 1939 it was the Brooklyn Dodgers and the Cincinnati Reds.

David "Suitcase" Cone doing what he does best.

Mountain Landis, the commissioner of baseball at the time, made a big important decision: No girls allowed — baseball is too difficult for the weaker sex.

COMMITMENT: I know what you're thinking. A man trying to get a commitment? But it's true. Pitchers and catchers are always looking for commitments, pointing at third base, pointing at first, trying to get the umpires to say that the batter has "committed." In this case, the commitment was to swing the bat. If the batter has tried to pull out of a swing, but the bat has crossed the plate, he is said to have committed. Only the base umpire with the best view of the situation can decide, and since commitment is an appeal play, the umpire won't offer his opinion unless he's asked for it. (See also Appeal.) AKA: Going around, strike

COMPLETE GAME: As opposed to what? An incomplete game? No. Baseball language is very specific. A complete game means that the starting pitcher plays the entire game, whether it goes

Cooperstown, home of baseball's Hall of Fame and the American Dream.

nine innings or 19. In today's game, with all the relievers in the bull pen, a complete game is a rare occurrence.

CONE, DAVID: Whenever they need a picture of an average looking baseball player, they use David Cone. He's about as normal looking as they get. In my books, hired arms like Suitcase Dave Cone don't do too much for the game. One day he's your hero, the next time you see him he's playing for the other guys. Rumor has it that he hums while on the mound, "On the road again" Some people call him the only remaining "money pitcher" in the game. So what are all the other guys playing for, peanuts? (See also Ace; Money Player.)

COOPERSTOWN: A charming little town in upstate New York, home of baseball's Hall of Fame, and allegedly the place where baseball was invented. Baseball is full of mythology, but at least most of it is loosely based on facts. The Cooperstown myth isn't a myth at all, it's pure fantasy. The story you were probably taught at school is that some guy named Abner Doubleday invented baseball in Cooperstown. This story is a deliberate fabrication, and every dedicated fan should know it. Doubleday was a West Point graduate, a Civil War hero, and a great American. He was also conveniently dead when in 1907 a blue-ribbon commission decided they needed a war hero to stand in as the inventor of the game. Doubleday is never known to have ever played, innovated, or even uttered the word "baseball!" A baseball guy named Harold Peterson said it best: "Abner Doubleday didn't invent baseball; baseball invented Abner Doubleday."

COUNT: Without the count, nobody would have any idea what was going on. It is the crucible of a baseball game. Every at bat starts the same, but that's where the predictability ends. When the player steps in, there is no count. With the first pitch, the umpire starts the count: "0-1" for a strike, "1-0" for a ball. The "balls" are always first. (Surprised? We're not.) The highest count is 3 and 2; anything more is either a walk or an out. But that doesn't mean there can be only 6 pitches: There can be as many foul balls as the batter can manage. It's not uncommon to see a batter stretch a 3-2 count to a dozen pitches or more.

COUSIN: Did you learn to dance with your cousin?

Ladies DAY

My cousin Jack was a good-looking high-school senior, and I didn't have to apologize for stepping on his feet. And I knew that he wasn't going to try anything; in a word, he was not threatening. This is exactly what it means in baseball. A cousin is what you call a pitcher who dishes up just the sort of stuff you can hit.

CUBAN FORKBALL: It sounds like a piece of Castro's flatware. But you won't see any Cuban forkballs in American ballparks. Under the Helms-Burton Legislation of 1996 they were made illegal; any pitcher caught throwing one is liable to life in prison, or six months in the Iowa Baseball Confederacy. These nasty curve balls thrown by degenerate money launderers are still legal tender in Montreal and Toronto, but we're working on it.

CUP OF COFFEE: For the hard working minor-leaguer, this is the ultimate coffee break. When the big club's bench is weak due to injury, late season trading, or desperate management, the team will often turn to the farm clubs to look for some heroics. To the minor-leaguer, it's his ticket to the good life: five-star hotels, autograph seekers, and postgame champagne. If he hits for the cycle, steals a few bases, or strikes out the side in the last couple of innings, he may be looking at a career in the majors. If he goes down looking, gets caught stealing third, or walks in the winning run, he will probably be back on the buses before he can unpack his shaving kit. Sport has an apt expression for this brief flirtation with greatness: "I just came up for a 'cup of coffee.'"

DID YOU KNOW

That in 1919, eight Chicago White Sox players were bribed into deliberately losing the World Series? The "Black Sox Scandal," as it is now known, gave the Grand Olde Game a black eye from which it took many years to recover.

This is Dizzy Dean, not Daffy.

CUTOFF PLAY: I had a pair of jeans that looked fantastic, but only when I was standing still. I paid too much to throw them away, so I cut them off nine inches above the knee and never looked back. On the diamond, they are far too sophisticated to play in cutoffs, but they do have a cutoff play, and it's not that different. When there is more than one runner on base, and the ball is hit into the outfield, sometimes it would be suicide to try to get the lead runner. This is where the cutoff play comes in. The lead runner is water under the bridge, but they might be able salvage something by throwing the ball to another base, tagging or checking the other runners. It looks a bit shaggy, but it's better than throwing the ball away and giving up an unearned base.

CY YOUNG AWARD: I'd like to say that the Cy Young Award was a prize given to the player best able to hide cellulite and wrinkles, but it's not. It's an award given to the best pitcher of the year from each league and is named after some old guy who won a lot of ball games. Every year a committee of

Ladies DAY

sports writers chooses the best pitcher from the National League and the American League as the Cy Young Award winner. (See also, Paige, Satchel.)

CYCLE: A hitter who "bats for the cycle" does not win a new Raleigh mountain bike, though he should win something. Hitting for the cycle means that a player has hit a single, a double, a triple, and a home run in the same game.

DEAN, DIZZY: Don't laugh. The guy was a great pitcher. He's in the Hall of Fame. He wasn't the smartest guy on the bench, but he wasn't daffy. That was his brother, Daffy Dean. In 1934, The St. Louis Cardinals won 95 games, and the Dean brothers, Dizzy and Daffy, won more than half of them. Dizzy won 30 and Daffy won 19. Do you feel like you're in a Saturday morning cartoon here?

DELAYED DOUBLE STEAL: Have you ever heard of the sleeping rabbit steal? Like the tango, not everybody can do it. The ones to watch are the sinewy little guys who like to smile too much. Watch Ricky Henderson, for example. He's on first base, dancing a few feet out from the bag, and the pitcher throws strike two. Henderson turns back toward first base and just as the catcher returns the ball to the pitcher's mound, Henderson spins on his heels and flies to second base. The pitcher has to wait for the ball, catch it in his glove, transfer it to his throwing hand, turn around, and throw a fastball to second base. If the runner is Ricky Henderson, he'll probably make it. If he doesn't time it right, though, he's no sleeping rabbit, he's a dead duck. In the delayed double steal, Ricky Henderson is stealing second while Paul Molitor is stealing third. This is not hard to watch.

> **? DID YOU KNOW**
>
> *That until 1996 Comiskey Park in Chicago, home of the White Sox, was the oldest ballpark in the big leagues? It opened in 1910 and was named after the team's owner, Charles Comiskey.*

Diamonds are a girls BEST FRIEND

Rose Gacioch

Rose Gacioch wasn't exactly a rookie when she joined the All American Girls Base Ball League. Gacioch had played for the last of the Bloomer Girls teams, and made the move to the new league with the ease of a seasoned professional. But she'd been around baseball long enough to pick up some bad language and was dispatched from the South Bend Blue Sox on account of her less than lady-like chatter. Rosie was signed by the Rockford Peaches in 1945, and stationed in right field, where nobody could hear her, and she set a league record in put-outs (*and* in put-downs...) Once her mouth was under control, she was moved to the infield, where she set records on the pitchers mound, first base and third.

DELIBERATE WALK: My friend Julia, the model, has a deliberate walk. But she gets paid for her deliberate walk. Julia looks ridiculous mincing around with her flawless hair and her perfect fingernails, swinging to the rhythm of her wiggle. But she's walking up a runway, not down to first base! And baseball has deliberate walks, too. It looks a bit stupid for the pitcher to throw four balls way out where the batter couldn't possibly hit them and the catcher to be standing back there with his arm extended. The purpose of this strange maneuver is to allow the batter to get to first base without having to do any work. Sometimes, if you make the guy work too hard for it, he'll head downtown on ya. Sometimes I think he should take Julia with him.

DEM BUMS: Considering the body-hugging uniforms worn by today's highly paid hunks, we might call *any* team Dem Bums. *Butt* seriously, it was the hapless Brooklyn Dodgers of the dirty thirties who were nicknamed "Dem Bums" by their perennially disappointed fans.

DESIGNATED HITTER: You'd think they were all designated hitters, wouldn't you? I mean, that's what they're designated to do when they stand there with a bat on their shoulders. But the designated hitter, or "DH," is like the stunt man for the pitcher. Everybody knows that pitchers are lousy hitters. In the American League, they recognize this fact, and so they've got a guy who doesn't have to play in the field, he just goes to bat. And though he's called the designated hitter, he doesn't hit the ball more often than anybody else. Go figure.

DIAMOND: If you go to the ballpark and all you

DID YOU KNOW

That in August 1920, a big-league ball player was killed in a game? Cleveland shortstop Ray Chapman was beaned by pitcher Carl Mays of the New York Yankees. Chapman died the following day of injuries received in the game.

see is a bunch of guys standing around a square, you're just lacking perspective. After all, what is a diamond but a square from another angle. It's like when he gave you that ring and said he'd love you forever — and you took it to 5th Avenue for an appraisal. Diamonds may be a girl's best friend, but romance requires a little imagination.

D*I*MAGGIO, JOE: Also known as Mr. Marilyn Monroe, "Joltin" Joe may have had an eye for blondes, but let's face it, he wasn't too bright. The career New York Yankee said, "I can remember being asked for a quote, and I didn't know what a quote was. I though it was some kind of soft drink." An American legend in his own time, The Yankee Clipper had it all: A career .325 average and Marilyn Monroe.

DINGER: It goes with hum, as in hum dinger, or it goes without. In either case, it empties the bases. (See also Home Run.)

DOBY, LARRY: If you don't know who Jackie Robinson is, look him up anywhere. If you don't know who Larry Doby is, don't feel bad. Nobody else does either. Larry Doby was the other first black man to play in the majors. When Doby joined the Cleveland Indians in 1947, Jackie Robinson had already broken the "color barrier," but Doby was the only black man playing in the American League. Doby didn't get the headlines, but he got the numbers. He hit .301 in his first full season and led the Cleveland Indians to the World Series with a .318 average. He also played on six consecutive all-star teams. So why doesn't everybody know who he was?

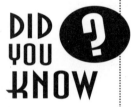

DID YOU KNOW

That Lou Brock of the St. Louis Cardinals stole 938 bases - without ever stealing home plate? A record for stealing. How original.

DOG DAYS: The period of time in the baseball season between August and September when fatigue from heavy heat and heavy scheduling begins to affect the team's performance. It's not that your ball-playing pooch is not hungry, it's just that he's too pooped to pounce.

DOUBLE: In life, maybe nothing is better than single. In baseball, double is definitely better than single. Getting to second base on a hit ball is a double, unless there is a fielding error. In that case, the runner is on second base but gets credit for a single, which is almost as good. Ball players are like most men; they don't pay much attention to whether anything or anybody is single.

DOUBLE PLAY: Seeing the guys "turn two" is one of the best things about watching a ball game. Usually, the defending team has a good chance of getting one of the outs, but the second usually requires more than one player stretching his skills to the limit to get the other one. There are quite a few ways for a double play to happen, but my favorite is around the horn. (See also Around the Horn; Turn Two.)

DOUBLEDAY, ABNER: The alleged inventor of baseball. Whatever anybody tells you, Abner Doubleday never had anything to do with

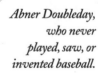

Abner Doubleday, who never played, saw, or invented baseball.

inventing baseball. He was probably a great guy — I mean he's named "Abner" for crying out loud, what do you expect? — he was a Civil War hero and all, but he never even *played the game* let alone invented it, as some people will tell you. If anybody tells you Abner Doubleday invented baseball, they need some tutoring. In fact, buy them a copy of this book. (See also Cartright, Alexander; Cooperstown.)

DOUBLEHEADER: This can be unspeakably boring. Like a date with both Ralph from the mailroom *and* Jeff from administration. On the other hand, for a real baseball fan, it can be like winning a small lottery. When a game is rained out, or otherwise called off, the game has to be made up later. The next time these two teams meet, they will have for play two games on the same day. If you're up to six or seven hours of baseball, a doubleheader may be just the ticket. (See also Nightcap.)

DOWN THE MIDDLE: This is just where baseball hitters like it. Sometimes it comes in a little high, a little low, or a little inside and they'll go for it anyway. But if it's right down the middle, they try to hit it out of the park. Down the middle is a pitching location, also known as down the pipe.

DRAFT: Aside from the watered-down beer they sell at the concession stands, there are other drafts in baseball. It's how they choose the players. Scouts travel around the country, and create a long list of hopeful hitters, hurlers and hustlers. On the day of the draft, these kids wait by their phones, hoping for a call from the Bigs. If the call comes, the kid becomes that team's property. It's like an arranged marriage, for Pete's sake. The players have no say in who chooses them, and they're in it for better or for worse. If the team tells the kid to spend the next three years playing right field in the Outer Dakota League, he'd better get used to life in the Badlands. And in that case, he's gonna need some of that other draft we were talking about.

DRAG BUNT: If the batter dressed in an outrageous evening gown, wore high heels, and bunted along third, this would definitely be a drag bunt. But the guy would have so many fellows chasing him around the clubhouse, he'd live to regret it. When the batter taps the ball with the bat and draws it toward first base with him, it's called a drag bunt. On the other hand, from the perspective of the third baseman, any bunt that gets the batter aboard is a drag.

DRIVE IN: America is a drive-in country. We've got drive-in movies, drive-in restaurants; we've even got drive-in churches! What a ball player wants is to drive in runs. (See also Ducks on the Pond; RBI.)

DROPPED THIRD STRIKE: I know this is when I would drop a guy: Three strikes and you're out! But sometimes, the guy gets a reprieve. If the batter strikes out, you will notice that the umpire will not call him out if the catcher misses the ball, or if the third strike hits the ground before being caught by the catcher. He doesn't call the batter "Out," because

? DID YOU KNOW

That 1982 marks the first time the Major League All-Star Game was played outside the United States? The Montreal Expos played host.

45
A-Z

he's not. If the catcher does not catch the third strike in the air, it doesn't matter whether the batter swung or not: He's not out until he is either tagged, or thrown out at first. If the third strike gets past the catcher, watch for the runner to "steal" first base!

DUCKS ON THE POND: What pond? I've seen ponds on the golf course, but I've never seen a water hazard on a baseball diamond! Batters hunt for ducks on the pond. They count up the number of runners already on the bases and figure that it should be easy work to bring them home with one good shot over the left-field wall. These guys should remember what my mother told me: Don't count your chickens before they're hatched. Chickens can't swim. (See also RBI.)

DUGOUT: Imagine a small room where 25 young guys with millions of dollars sit around drinking. OK, forget it. The picture that comes to mind is probably about the furthest thing imaginable from the room I'm thinking about. In the dugout, the millionaires only wear pinstripes if they play for the Yankees, and they spit Gatorade and chewing tobacco all over the floor. The dugout is where all the players sit while they're waiting for a turn at bat.

DUSTER: Baseball is obsessed with housework. Half the things players do sound like household chores

DID YOU KNOW ?

That the first game played under the lights at Chicago's Wrigley's Field was played by two women's all-star teams in 1943 — forty years before the men played under the Southside starlight?

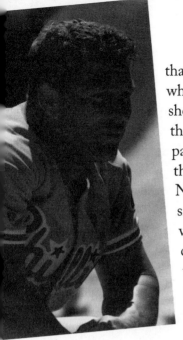

Lenny Dyksta isn't happy.

that your mother taught you when you were a kid. But did she tell you that if you did them well, somebody would pay you $4.5 million over three years to do them? Neither did mine. It's no small wonder they're obsessed with housework though, they do everything possible to get themselves and everybody else as dirty as possible. The duster, for example, is a pitch intended to make the batter dive into the dust beside home plate. (See also Chin Music.)

DYKSTRA, LENNY: Watch Lenny Dykstra at the plate. He doesn't look like he's ready to play baseball, he looks more like he's going fishing. If you look up "open stance" in a baseball dictionary, they'll have a picture of Lenny Dykstra. But don't underestimate this boy on account of his casual style; Dykstra can play ball!

EARLY BLOOMER: Remember Cindy, the girl in your science class who had a body like a soap opera starlet when

Lenny Dyksta making everybody happy.

The fabled Elysian Fields, where baseball was born.

you were still hoping for a training bra? These guys are the same. I don't mean they ended up in the suburbs with four kids and a deadbeat husband; I mean they start off the season with too many home runs and extra-base hits. Talk about creating disastrous expectations! Just like Cindy, they're left with little to do for an encore.

ELYSIAN FIELDS: I don't know why they had to invent Abner Doubleday and the story of how he invented the game of baseball in Cooperstown, New York. The real story is better. In New York of the 1840s, there was public parkland on the shores of the Hudson River known as the Elysian Fields. On misty summer Sunday mornings, bankers, lawyers, and stock promoters would gather there to refine the game that was sweeping the nation.

There were many versions of the new game being tried from Sunday to Sunday, but the one that won out was Alexander Cartwright's Base Ball. (See also Cooperstown; Doubleday, Abner.)

ERA: Earned run average. The smaller the ERA, the better the pitcher. The ERA tells you the average number of runs the pitcher allows in nine innings. To calculate a pitcher's ERA, take the total number of earned runs scored against him, multiply by nine, then divide by the number of innings pitched. For example, if the pitcher has given up 10 earned runs and pitched 30 innings, you multiply 10 runs by nine (10 x 9 = 90) and divide by the number of innings pitched (90 ÷ 30 = 3.00). The pitcher's ERA is 3.00. The ERA was also an amendment to the American Constitution giving

> **DID YOU KNOW**
>
> *That the pitcher's rubber is considered to be* a foreign substance? *If a ball were to bounce on the rubber and bounce outside the foul lines, it would be considered a foul ball!*

Diamonds are a girls BEST FRIEND

LIZZIE ARLINGTON

Lizzie Arlington holds a unique place in the history of baseball. She was the first woman to find herself playing on a men's professional team. It wasn't that the professional teams of the time didn't allow women to play - that prohibition came later - it was just that nobody had ever done it before!

Arlington was paid 100 dollars a week to pitch for the Philadelphia Reserves; quite a tidy sum in 1898! And though she lived up to her reputation as an ace pitcher, she wasn't bringing the crowds to the park, and was let go before the season closed. Edward Barrow, president of the Atlantic League, believed that the novelty of a female player would bring in the fans and signed Lizzie Arlington to a minor league contract. She was good, but not good enough, and when the honeymoon was over, baseball's first female professional moved down the road to the Bloomer Girls system.

women equal rights with men. The only people working harder than major-league pitchers to reduce the ERA were Bible Belt Republicans. In both cases, less is more.

ERROR: Guys who get paid the kind of money baseball players do are not supposed to make mistakes. When they do, they are charged with an error. If they boot a ball, make a lousy throw to first, or let an easy double-play ball scoot out of the infield, they hardly ever get away with it; somebody's always keeping score. (See also Alibi Ike; Official Scorer.)

EXCUSE ME: Baseball can be very polite. Sometimes a batter starts his swing, then changes his mind at the last second. If he can't quite get the bat out of the way, he makes contact with the ball and sends it past the infield by mistake. "Excuse me" isn't something the batter says to the first baseman, it's something the announcers call the hit.

EXHIBITION GAME: This is unlike the exhibitionists' game, where all the players play naked. But in either case, the game doesn't count. An exhibition game is played for the fun of it (the Hall of Fame Game), for practice (a spring training game), or to show off (the All-Star Game). In any case, it's nearly as amusing as the exhibitionists' game.

EXPANSION: This is what happens to ball players who spend too much time relaxing over the winter. It's also what happens to the league when the owners decide that they can make more money by letting some new teams into the game. Since expansion teams don't have an established farm system, or management or corporate structure, they are not

DID YOU KNOW

That in 1993, for the first time in 100 years, three players from the same team finished 1-2-3 at the top of the American League's batting standings? The World Series winning Toronto Blue Jays boasted the top three hitters: John Olerud (.363), Paul Molitor (.332), and Roberto Alomar (.326).

Ty Cobb (sliding) was said to go everywhere with a million dollars in cash on him. We wonder if he brought the money to third base.

expected to do very well in their first few years. So expansion is also an excuse young teams use to account for their poor showing in the standings.

FAIR BALL: In determining the "fairness of a ball," they don't weigh it, measure it, or see how it reacts in situations involving danger. If the ball travels within the bounds of the baselines and ends up inside the foul poles, it's a fair ball.

FAN INTERFERENCE: In ballpark etiquette, fan interference ranks right up there with bringing a parasol to the ballyard. If the ball comes anywhere near you, and you're in the front row, don't touch it. If you interfere with the play, two guys in suits will come and escort you from the ballpark, and they won't listen to anything you have to say.

FANNED: We all know it gets hot in the ballpark, but in this day and age, they could at least get air conditioning! The pitcher causes the fanning, though, and these guys are stingy. They whip those balls so fast that the batter has to start his swing in the stretch to get the bat on anything more solid than fresh air, which is where the fanning comes in. (See also Stretch; Whiff.)

FARM: The farm is where they grow baseball players. They take fresh scrubbed kids, give them the sort of fertilizer you would expect, and weed out the boys who can't take the heat. Long bus rides, lousy pay, and hot summer days in no-name towns are the dues minor-leaguers have to pay before finding themselves in the big show and the big money.

FELLER, BOB: Did you know anybody in high school who was remarkable? I went to school with Arnold Raftek. He won the interstate chess championship. Impressed? Well, Bob Feller might have impressed you. When he was a 17-year-old-high school sophomore, he took a summer job with the Cleveland Indians in 1936 and struck out 15 batters in his first major-league start. The next game he struck out 17. He won five games, lost three, and went home to Iowa to harvest his dad's crops and finish his senior year. I wonder if he had any trouble getting a date for the harvest dance? When Feller finally got serious about baseball, he played for 20 years, pitching three no-hitters and twelve one-hitters. Feller also wound up with a 3.25 ERA.

? DID YOU KNOW

That the legendary Ty Cobb holds the all-time record for stealing home? He did it 35 times. Now, let's put this into some perspective. When Cobb stole a base, he did it with his razor-sharp spikes aimed at the other guy's face. He was probably responsible for more cuts and stitches than any man in baseball. So how many catchers want to stand in the way of Ty Cobb on a suicide play?

A-Z

DID YOU KNOW?

That the Philadelphia Phillies hold the record for the worst choke in history? In 1964, with only 11 games left in the regular season, they were ahead by six-and-a-half games and managed to finish the season in second place out of the play-offs.

FIELDER'S CHOICE: So what are they choosing between, takeout Chinese food or pizza? Not a chance. The fielder is choosing between throwing out the runner who is already on base or the guy who hit the ball. Given the choice, he'll get the runner every time. But when he can't get the man moving into scoring position, he settles for the batter. In that case, it's probably a sacrifice. A fielder's choice doesn't count as a hit, and the batter doesn't get credit for it if he makes it to first base.

FLAIR: Flair is not the style with which the players curve the bill of their caps, nor is it the cut of their longstockings; a flair is a ball hit between the infield and the outfield. But like a winning style, a flair has a good chance of getting a guy to first base! If he's from the south, he might call it a Texas leaguer. If he's from the west, he might call it a short poke. If he's lucky, he'll call it a base hit.

FLIPPER: Did you ever see the episode where Flipper saves a whole school of killer whales? It's nothing like that. A flipper is just one more word for describing the guy at the center of the game — the pitcher. (See also Pitcher.)

FLOOD, CURT: Every night, when baseball players kneel down next to their beds and say their prayers, they always include a blessing for Curt Flood. Baseball owners, and many fans, on the other hand (or knee), call him names we don't want to print here. And they all do it for the same reason. And it wasn't because he was such a great outfielder. Baseball remembers Curt Flood because he was the guy who took Major League Baseball to the U.S. Supreme Court where he challenged the

Diamonds are a girls BEST FRIEND

SOPHIE KURYS

'The Flint Flash', Sophie Kurys, was just a kid when she joined up with the Racine Belles of the All American Base Ball League, and there was no stopping her. In fact, there was no *catching* her. At 5'5" and 120 pounds, Sophie didn't look like much of a threat to anybody, but it didn't take long for Belles' manager Johnny Gottselig to realize what sort of talent he had running the bases. In 1943, she stole 44 times. In '44, she stole 166. By 1946, when she was just 21 years old, she was leading the league in two categories: walking and running. She walked to first base a remarkable 93 times, and once she got there, she was a cinch to steal second. And third. Sophie reached base 215 times and stole 201 bases in 203 attempts, a record no major leaguer has ever come close to breaking. In major league circles, Rickey Henderson, who stole 130 bases in 1982, is regarded as the game's greatest base thief, but Henderson doesn't do it in a skirt and bare legs. And even in his regulation uniform, he can't hold a candle to Sophie Kurys.

hated Reserve Clause. Flood lost the challenge, and he never made the kind of money today's superstars see, but he opened the floodgates that sent the revenue stream straight into the pockets of the people who play the game. (See also Reserve Clause.)

FORCE-OUT: Think of baserunning as line-dancing with umpires. On the dance floor you might feel stupid if you don't jump when the music says jump, but nobody makes you go sit down! It's more like musical chairs. When a batter hits a fair ball, he has to go to first base. If there's already somebody at first, the guy at first had better get to second before the ball does, because he can't be at first base any more. If the ball gets there before the runner does, he has to go sit down. Forced out.

FOUL POLE: I knew a guy called Andy Gorski who swore and spit at every opportunity. He was a foul Pole, but he isn't the one I'm talking about. The foul poles are markers which extend the first and third baselines to map out the geometry of the ball diamond. They're usually painted yellow; you can't miss them. The foul pole decides whether a late inning wallop is a loud strike or a game-winning homer.

FOUR-PLY POKE: There are a lot of ways to say "home run" in baseball — the longball, downtowner, four bagger, round trip, homer, full circuit, slam, dinger — but "four-ply poke" has a certain charm for the sort of folks who call

---

DID YOU KNOW?

That the National Baseball Hall of Fame and Museum opened in Cooperstown, New York, in 1939? The idea was to commemorate the mythical invention of the game at Cooperstown in 1839. Of course nothing happened in Cooperstown in 1839 - they didn't invent the game, they invented the whole story!

Ladies DAY

the bat "lumber." I wonder what Martha Stewart calls it?

FREE AGENT: Just like the civil engineer, the free agent is an oxymoron. Free agents can be both, oxes and morons, that is. Julia has an agent. She's a model. When I told her that there were free agents in baseball she wanted to know where to sign up. Hers gets 15 percent for answering telephone calls. But a free agent isn't a negotiator who doesn't charge anything. A free agent is a guy who can make up his own mind what team he's gonna play for. His contract has expired, and all the trade clauses have been optioned out. No guy in no suit in no front office is gonna tell him what to do, no sir. He's a free agent. Instead, some guy in some suit at the agent's office is gonna tell him what to do. And the agent isn't free either. He charges about 15 percent for answering phone calls. Like I said, the free agent is an oxymoron.

FREE PASS: When the pitcher has to face some guy who's hitting .433 for his last 10 games and the tying run is on second base, he doesn't really want to throw anything the guy can hit. He may get a visit from the catcher, the manager, the pitching coach, or even the umpire. What they are all doing out there on the mound is arguing about the cost of a free pass. Are they going to take the chance and go for a strike out, or will they just "pitch around" the batter, throwing four unhittable balls to send the runner to first base? The cost of a free pass is putting another "duck on the pond" for the on deck man. (See also Deliberate Walk.)

FREE SWINGER: This has nothing to do with Baseball Annie or any of her friends. In fact it has nothing to do with liberal morality or the type of marriage arrangements the players have with their wives. Some guys stand there all day waiting for just the right pitch to come along, so they can hit the ball in exactly the right place. These guys are not what you call free swingers. If they stand there for too long, we call them "Out." (See also Freeze the Batter.) Free swingers try to hit almost anything they can reach. They don't care whether it's a corner-shaving split-fingered fastball or a Cuban forkball, they just take a whack at it. You'll never see a free swinger stand there and take strike three, but if the free swinger isn't also a very good hitter, you won't see him at all since he's probably playing right field somewhere in Nebraska. (See also Bush League.)

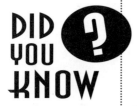

That Mark McGwire, the big-hitting rookie of the 1987 campaign, hit 49 home runs in his first big-league season? How long will it be before somebody tops that? Keep them Wheaties on the breakfast table, girl. You can be sure his mom isn't driving the old station wagon anymore.

FREEZE THE BATTER: Baseball may be a technically advanced game, but they haven't mastered cryogenics: Freezing the batter is what a pitcher hopes to do to a hitter who is playing the psychological game. It's an exercise in confusion. The pitcher might throw a fastball down the middle, followed by a low and inside breaking pitch, then an outside fastball. By this time, the batter doesn't know what to expect, and if his psychological framework is sufficiently shaken, the pitcher can "freeze" him with an unpredictable strike. The batter, trying to decide what the pitcher is up to, spends a split-second too long dithering while the ball smacks leather and the ump calls "Steerike!"

The one thing more American than watching baseball.

FRONT OFFICE: It's not any different in baseball than anywhere else. The guys in the front office are all guys, and they tell everybody else what to do. They have all the information, most of the money, and they make insane decisions that any regular in the bleachers knows are stupid. They'll trade your star center fielder for a left-handed pitcher with warts and two guys in the Dominican Republic, and the next year they'll give you a free calendar on opening day to make up for it. What do you expect from a bunch of overgrown cub scouts with money?

Diamonds are a girls BEST FRIEND

Amanda Clement

The Clement family were among the first settlers in the state of Dakota, so it's fitting that their daughter, Amanda was to stake a claim in the baseball history books. Hank Clement, Amanda's brother, was playing in a game between teams from Renville and Hawarden, and Amanda went along for the ride. When the umpire didn't show, Hank suggested that his kid sister could do the job. She'd been umpiring family games for years, and knew the game cold. With no obvious alternatives, they gave Amanda the nod and never looked back. They were so impressed they offered her the regular officiating job. Thus it was, in 1904, when Renville, Hawarden and Amanda Clement played their way into the history of the National Past Time. We don't know what happened to the boys from Renville and Hawarden, but the South Dakota Sports Hall of Fame remembers Clement as the first woman umpire ever inducted.

FROZEN ROPE: An Eskimo cowboy's lariat? A shoelace in a snowstorm? Nope. It's a line drive. (See also Clothesline.)

FULL COUNT: In the late, late movies, the Count isn't full till he's sucked everybody dry. In baseball, the full count (3 balls and 2 strikes) is something the pitcher has to encounter regularly. In the contest between a batter and a pitcher, the full count signals that the pussyfooting is all over. The pitcher has run out of options to tease; the batter has run out of chances to outguess the pitcher. The next pitch is the payoff. But the full count doesn't really mean it's all over but the counting. Several things can happen. The batter can hit the ball fair and get as many bases as he's able, he can strike out (swinging or looking), he can "take" ball four and go to first base (see also Base on Balls), or he can foul off as many 3 and 2 pitches as the pitcher serves up. (See also Count.)

FUNGO: Where do they get these names? It sounds like something you should wear rubber gloves to scrub the bathroom with. Baseball encyclopedias agree on one thing about fungo — nobody knows where the name comes from. Fungo is what all the kids do in the park: One guy hits fly balls and the other guys catch them. Major-leaguers do the same thing as a warm-up before games sometimes. In fact, many parks have a fungo circle, where the guy with the bat stands, and he uses a fungo bat designed to hit very high fly balls. I'm not kidding.

GAEDEL, EDDIE: Eddie Gaedel is the answer to the trivia question which goes something like: "Who was the shortest man to play Major League

DID YOU KNOW?

That baseball became an official Olympic medal sport at the 1992 Summer Olympics in Barcelona, Spain?

Baseball?" In 1951, St. Louis owner Bill Veeck had Gaedel jump out of a cake in a Browns uniform. Gaedel, who had a legal contract with the team, for the day, came to the plate to the hoots and jeers of players and fans alike. At 3 feet 7 inches tall, Gaedel had a strike zone so small they would have needed a microscope to find it. Once at first base, on balls, they sent in a guy with longer legs to run the bases.

GAMES BEHIND: This is not the top tush of the evening; this is where your team is unless it's in first place. If they're not the league leader, they are some number of games behind. A win or a loss is worth half a game, and who you're playing with can be very important in the homestretch. But like your winter wardrobe, nobody really cares about "games behind" in the summer. By the time September closes in, there will be plenty of time to worry about how many games behind you are. Relax, enjoy the season. When they start talking about "games behind" on the radio, that's a sure sign that it's time to take your winter coat to the cleaners.

GAP: Like the space between David Letterman's teeth, this gap is open for trouble. The gap, or alley, is the spot between the two outfielders where a sharply hit ball can drop safely. The size and location of the gap changes, depending on the speed of the fielders, the velocity of the ball, and the team's dental plan.

GARDEN: The outfield. Also known as the pasture or the orchard, the garden is no place to loaf around and pick daisies. The gardener is expected to catch any flies that buzz out his way. Whatever

Lou Gehrig and Babe Ruth. Murderers in their striped uniforms.

you find in your shed, you can find in baseball: A lawnmower is a sharply hit ground ball; a weed eater is the same as a lawnmower only it moves faster. A garden weasel is a squibber that gets behind an outfielder. If the outfielder is Alibi Ike, he'll blame the weasel.

GEHRIG, LOU: If it hadn't been for Babe Ruth, Lou Gehrig would have been the greatest player of his day. What you need to know about him is that he

DID YOU KNOW?

That Joe DiMaggio rubbed his with olive oil; Germany Schaefer bit his to get a better grip; Honus Wagner boiled his in linseed oil; Babe Ruth liked his to be knotty; Joe Jackson slept with his? Of course we're talking about their lucky bats. What did you think?

played more consecutive games than anybody but Cal Ripkin and that they named a terrible disease after him. The number of consecutive games played was 2,130, and the fatal disease was amyotrophic lateral sclerosis (Lou Gehrig's disease) which took him from the playing field to death's door in just two dreadful years.

GETTING TO FIRST BASE: The thing that's uppermost on the guy's mind. So what else is new. If he's going to score, he's got to get to first base. Baseball recognizes the importance of this to these eager swingers, so they give them seven different ways to get there: a base hit, a base on balls, an error, a fielder's choice, a dropped third strike, catcher interference, or being hit by a pitch. I'd give them about half as many chances as this.

GILLETTE: The man who invented the disposable razor was a bottle cap salesman named King Gillette, and though he was a great fan of the game, he probably never dreamed they'd name a hit after him!

GO DOWN LOOKING: You know this scene: You're walking along in your new pumps and best suit, and you're feeling as good as you look. But you're not looking where you're going. You don't see that patch of ice on the sidewalk. As you fall, gracefully, of course, you go down looking to see who's watching. In baseball, if you go down looking, you've wasted your last chance. When the batter stands there while strike three whistles past him, he goes down looking. (See also Free Swinger.)

GO THE DISTANCE: Men brag about being able to

Diamonds are a girls BEST FRIEND

JEAN FAUT

Jean Faut was born to play baseball, and she was born at just the right time and place to do it. As a high school senior in Greeneville Pennsylvania, Faut was already a regular on and off the semi pro diamonds, having attended games all her life and pitched in exhibitions. When the All American Girls Base Ball League gave her a try out, she landed a spot as a third baseman for the South Bend Blue Sox franchise. By 1949, she had been moved to the pitcher's mound, where she belonged, and in 1951 pitched the league's first perfect game. The league's Player of the Year for 1951, Faut took the winter off to have a baby, and was back on the mound in time for spring training. In 1953, Jean was back to full form, and pitched a second perfect game, though she did not take the winter off to have another baby. She retired from the game. As the wife of the team's manager, Karl Winsch, the pressure was too much for her to handle. Faut could throw a fastball, a screw ball and a curve ball. The only thing she couldn't handle was the stress of being the bosses wife.

Ken Griffey Junior. If the hat fits...

DID YOU KNOW?

That four sets of twins played major-league ball? None of them ever played for Minnesota. Too bad.

Ladies DAY

go the distance. But what's the big deal? In the old days, a pitcher might be expected to play 100 games a year; and when he started a game, he was expected to finish it, unless he got hurt. Today's high-priced talent might start 40 games in a year and go the distance a couple of times. Big deal. My friend Gloria's husband does about the same, and she complains about it.

GOLDEN GLOVE AWARD: The Golden Glove Award is not a pair of Betty Crocker oven mitts handed out for the season's lightest pastry — though the winner is definitely a dough boy come contract time. Golden Gloves are awarded to the player who excels beyond all others in each of the fielding positions. Both the National and American Leagues award Golden Gloves at each position.

GRAND SLAM: A home run with the bases loaded. I've heard big talk about men who take four women home and satisfy them all at the same time. Only in the daytime dramas, you say? Well, sure, except in baseball, where with one swipe of his bat, a lucky slugger can bring home four players and satisfy an entire stadium full of women *and* men.

GREEN LIGHT: A green light is a message to the batter. It means the same thing as when you smile demurely at your beau: "Go ahead, give it your best shot." When a hitter has three balls and no strikes, he is probably given the red light signal from the manager: "Don't swing — one more bad pitch and you're on your way to first base." When the manager has enough confidence in a batter, though, he might give him the green light in such a situation. You see, it's not that different at all. (See also Red Light.)

GRIFFEY, KEN, JUNIOR: Junior. I've never understood why a grown man would want to call himself "Junior." Take Griffey for example. He's one of the greatest hitters of the '90s, he makes more money than the president of General Motors, and people call him Junior. I wonder if Robert Bly would have anything to say about this.

GROUND BALL: Like ground beef, it's a staple. Mixed with just the right spice, a batter can turn an ordinary grounder into a base hit.

GROUND RULES: It's always a good idea to have them clear before you start playing ball. If there is no way that you're going to do more than go to dinner, you let your date know straight off. The same thing happens in baseball. Before the game, the managers and the umpire meet at home plate and go over the

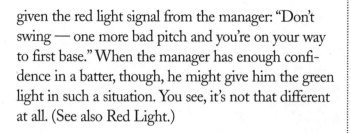

Ken Griffey Junior with his hat on the right way around.

Rickey Henderson, the greatest leadoff hitter of all time.

ground rules for that particular park. That way, there are no embarrassing misunderstandings. You see, except for the strange language, baseball isn't that different from life.

GWINN, TONY: This guy might look like the Michelin Man, but he uses those spare tires to roll over the four-base track. Every pitcher in the National League is afraid of Gwinn who consistently hits .335. In San Diego, where he's played for the Padres since 1982, they just call him Papa.

HAM AND EGG RELIEVER: I don't know what your kids get for dinner on your night out, but in my house, I bring in my ham and egg reliever.

Ladies DAY

They get all the basics, and they eat it all up. At the ballpark, you call in a ham and egg reliever when you need a pitcher who's not gonna put pepper on everything and get it spit right back at him. He's got a good fastball, maybe a curve or two, and he can take you right into the late innings. (See also Long Man.)

HANGING CURVE: Unless you're a batter, it's a bad thing. When my friend Julia, the model, has hanging curves, she jogs and eats carrot sticks. Now, having curves is as de rigueur on the pitchers mound as on the catwalk, but if they get out of control, you're done for. When a pitcher throws a curve ball that doesn't curve, it kind of just sits there, making a pretty juicy target for the guy with the stick. Too many hanging curves will get a pitcher whacked out of the lineup as quickly as Julia will be whisked off the runway.

HENDERSON, RICKEY: Arguably the most successful leadoff hitter in baseball, Henderson is also a contender for the largest ego award. Rickey can hit, bunt, run, steal, and throw as well as anybody in baseball. If you're going to a game where Henderson is playing, get tickets along the third-base

? DID YOU KNOW

That Caesar Cedeno, who was a shoe-in for the Hall of Fame, saw his career crumble in 1973 when a woman was found shot to death in his hotel room. Cedeno was never charged, but the baseball honchos are less forgiving than the Dominican police department.

Rickey Henderson telling everyone that he is the greatest leadoff hitter of all time.

side for the best view of his batting stance. If you want to talk to him, sit in the left-field corner; he loves to chat with the fans while he's out shagging fly balls.

HENTGEN, PAT: In an age where starting pitchers refuse to play when Jo-Jo the psychic warns of an ominous night or because they got a callous carrying their club bag into the hotel, this Cy Young winning pitcher is a manager's dream come true. Pat Hentgen has never missed a start in his entire major-league career. In 1996, on his 28th birthday, he was named the American League's best pitcher. Where did he get this remarkable work ethic? It might have something to do with his Motor City (Detroit) roots. Gentlemen, start your engines.

HIDDEN BALL TRICK: The hidden ball trick hardly ever works, but when it does, it's mortifying. Last month, I called in sick and headed downtown for a radical haircut. The next morning I came breezing in sporting blonde curls and found a note from the boss on my desk: "Sheila called from Hair Unbelievable: You are confirmed for 11:45. Does Sheila have a remedy for a cold? See me." The hidden ball trick is a little like that. The runner is so full of himself after hitting safely, that he's not paying attention. The first baseman still has the ball hidden in his glove, and the runner steps off the bag. Surprise! He's out!

HIGH HARD ONE: An overzealous drunk who can't control his urges? Nope. A high hard one is a fastball right up under the batter's chin. A high hard one will be a bean ball if the batter doesn't watch out. (See also Chin Music.)

DID YOU KNOW?

That not only the batter but the bat gets a shave before the game? To reduce the weight of the bat, players like to shave a little wood off of the handle, making the bat easier to swing. But just like Samson, taking a little too much off will make it weaker and liable to shatter on contact.

Toronto's Pat Hentgen, Cy Young Award winner.

Diamonds are a girls BEST FRIEND

Alta Weiss

Dr. George Weiss had an eye for talent, a remarkably modern understanding of women, and bags of money. When his daughter Alta needed to go to high school, he built her one, when she needed a place to play, he built a baseball stadium, and later, when she had proved herself on the diamond, he bought her what every American girl should have: A team of her own. Alta hadn't wasted her natural or her paternal gifts, and excelled at baseball, and at thinking. When on holiday at the family lodge on Lake Erie, the local mayor spotted Weiss playing catch with some of the local players, and signed her on the spot. The fortunes of the Vermillion Independents (an otherwise all male team) took an immediate turn for the better. Train loads of eager fans arrived to see Girl Wonder in action. The next season, Daddy bought her a semi-pro team, the Weiss All Stars, where he could show-case his little girl and rake in the cash himself. As the summers passed, Alta played less and less frequently, turning her attention towards her education. In 1914 she graduated as a Doctor of Medicine, and not surprisingly, was the only female in the class.

HIT BY PITCH: My friend Julia is always being hit on. She's beautiful and very single so she hears a lot of pitches. When she's struck by one, the guy usually gets to first base, maybe further if he's playing the game by her rules. When a batter gets hit by a pitch, it doesn't matter how well it was delivered, or where it hit him, he only gets to first base.

HOLD THE RUNNER: I've got a few girlfriends who are experts at this. Most of the runners they're holding I'd let walk, but that's their business, not mine. For pitchers it doesn't matter whether the guy's got a face like a hound dog or a body like Superman, he's got to do what he can to hold the runner. How does he do it? About the same way my friends do it. He pays a lot more attention to the runner than he deserves. He watches him out of the corner of his eye, throws the ball to the base to keep him close, and tries to intimidate him into staying put. If the pitcher doesn't pay enough attention to the runner, the guy is very liable to start running the minute the pitcher "goes home" with the ball. (See also Steal.)

THE HOLE: When I was at college, there was a room in my dorm that was so small they didn't assign it to anybody. We called it "the hole." When somebody's date got way past first base, they would sheepishly emerge from the hole at sunrise, looking tired and wanting breakfast. In baseball, if you hit into the hole, you might get to second base, but you won't get breakfast. The hole is the undefended area of the infield just beyond the range of the fielders.

HOLLYWOOD PLAY: Let's face it, baseball is entertainment. But some of these guys just can't

> **? DID YOU KNOW**
>
> *That the youngest man to ever play major-league ball was not a man at all? At 15 years old, Joe Nuxhall wasn't old enough to hold a drivers license, much less vote!*

DID YOU KNOW?

That prior to 1946, black players were not allowed to be signed to major-league clubs? Jackie Robinson was the first black man to play major-league baseball in modern times. Robinson broke the color barrier when he signed with the Montreal Royals in 1946 and came up to the big club with the Brooklyn Dodgers the following season. We wonder when the first woman will break the gender barrier.

resist the urge to make a routine play look like a monumental event. You know the guys we mean, the ones who slide headfirst into third base when the ball is still in right field. Or the guys who jump and pivot to make a routine line drive look like a gold medal achievement. Ball Park Franks; hotdogs. We expect Sly Stallone to overact. That's his job. But on the diamond, we expect to see it played straight: Real life, real drama.

HOME PLATE: Just like Dorothy said, "There's no place like home." They called it home because it's where it all begins, and where it all ends. And you know who cleans home plate? The umpire! Really. He keeps a little broom in his back pocket, and when the plate gets dirty, he makes a big production out of sweeping it off. I mean, what's the big deal? Does anybody think it matters if the plate is dirty? Is it worth stopping the game while 50,000 people wait for you to clean up? Talk about obsessive behavior!

HOME RUN: Why do they call it a home run? I don't know. Once the ball goes over the fence, it doesn't matter whether the guy runs, walks, or crawls around the bases; they can't get him out! But baseball has etiquette. If the batter walks or trots around the bases, he is making a point; he is showing up the pitcher. He is saying "Thanks for the free ride, cousin." He can expect a bean ball next time at bat.

HOOVER: Why are these guys obsessed with housework? Weed eaters, clotheslines, lawn mowers...They wouldn't know the difference between a clothesline and a broom. They call a

74

Ladies DAY

sharply hit grounder a hoover since you can pick up a hit with it. They also call a shortstop a hoover if he vacuums up any ground balls hit in his bailiwick. So why don't they call a guy a garbage disposal when he eats up the junk tossed his way by an action pitcher?

HOT CORNER: In my hometown, the hot corner is the place most men don't admit that they have ever frequented. There's a hot corner in baseball too, and it's a place you don't want your line drive to end up. The hot corner is third base, so named for the sharply hit balls that are smashed into the zone.

HUMPBACK LINER: My aunt Marta in the swimming pool. In baseball, it's a line drive without the speed of a frozen rope — sort of a cross between a Texas leaguer and a clothes line.

ICE-CREAM CONE: Ice-cream cones are one of the joys of baseball. And they're not just available at the snack bar; they're being served up on the field, too! But the players hate 'em. It's what baseballers call a catch where the ball sticks out of the tip of the fielder's glove, like, well, like an ice-cream cone. The fielder doesn't particularly like it because it's just a little too close for comfort; the batter doesn't like it because it represents an out when he was looking for an extra-base hit. But fans love it because it shows us the fine line between winning and losing.

IN THE BOOKS: An official baseball game is nine innings long or longer. Somebody always wins, somebody always loses. But if the big

Guy upstairs (and we don't mean the commissioner of baseball) decides to send rain, wind, or a natural disaster to bring an early end to the contest, baseball has a way of dealing with it: Once five full innings have been played, the game is said to be in the books. Carved in stone.

INSIDE THE PARK HOME RUN: You don't see this very often; it happens only a couple of times a year, but it's something to see. Think about it, 52 teams each play 160 games, plus playoffs, and every game has at least 27 at bats per team (in fact the average is more like 41 at bats); and in the park home runs average about three per season. The odds run around 115,073-to-1 against it happening in any given situation. So don't count on seeing it too often. An in the park home run is exactly what the name says: It is a home run in which the ball does not leave the park. If the ball is hit high and hard and lands in a corner of the outfield, and if the runner's legs are stronger than the fielder's arm, sometimes the runner can run the full 360 feet around the base paths before the ball can be thrown home. It won't happen often, so if you see one, make it a Kodak moment.

INFIELD: Of the nine men on the field, six of them are infielders. The pitcher, catcher, first baseman, second baseman, shortstop, and third baseman are infielders. The other guys are outfielders. This is the defensive team.

INFIELD FLY RULE: Boys love to argue. Arguing about sports is what most of them are best at. The infield fly rule is about the most complicated rule you'll ever have to know, unless you want to be an

Diamonds are a girls BEST FRIEND

TONI STONE

This rolling stone never let any moss gather on her. Toni Stone was a determined young lady who just wanted to play the game. And play she did; in fact she played in the majors and was the first woman to do so.

Marcenia Lyle Alberga, her birth name, grew up in the 1930s, playing alongside the boys in her St. Paul, Minnesota, neighborhood, where she was considered one of the best. She earned the nickname Tomboy and with much persistence captured the attention of Gabby Street, former St. Louis Cardinal's manager, who coached a minor-league team in her hometown. Street also ran a baseball school, and Stone managed to prove her abilities and gained acceptance into the school.

In 1946, she changed her name to Toni Stone and moved south, having earned a spot on the San Francisco Sea Lions, an all-male black barnstorming team. Things were looking rosy, but, like her sister-in-arms, Lizzie Murphy, she soon found she was getting stiffed financially by the head office. So, when a better offer came from the New Orleans Creoles she took it. She would later join the ranks of the Indianapolis Clowns, where she took over second base from the departing Henry Aaron.

Stone played out her career in the Negro Leagues until her retirement in 1954. When the Baseball Hall of Fame finally honored the Negro League players in 1991, Stone was among them — the only woman.

This is proof the Shoeless Joe Jackson did, in fact, wear shoes.

umpire. If there are runners on first and second base (or if the bases are loaded) and less than two outs, the batter is automatically out if he hits a fly ball to the infield. Why? If the fielder lets the ball drop to the ground, or if he drops it accidentally on purpose, the runners are sitting ducks.

INNING: Not the opposite of an outing. An inning is six outs long — three for each team. It doesn't matter how long it takes or how many runs score.

A game is scheduled to have nine innings, no matter how long it takes. And it can take awhile. Some night games have ended up as morning games before a winner emerged.

JACKSON, JOE: It's too bad we remember Joe Jackson as one of the Chicago Black Sox. Shoeless Joe Jackson, who never played in his bare feet, was one of the greatest outfielders and extra-base hitters of his day. Jackson could maybe read his name in the headlines, but otherwise, he was illiterate. A guy behind third base once yelled out to Jackson, "How do you spell illiterate?" Jackson replied with a hit that got him all the way to third base. He sneered at the guy and hollered back, "Hey, bigmouth, how do you spell triple?"

JACKSON, REGGIE: You think today's players have big egos? That's just because you didn't know Reggie Jackson. The guy makes Jose Canseco look like Little Bo Peep. He once said that a pitcher "should be glad he'll be able to tell his grandchildren he once pitched to Reggie Jackson." And he said it when he was hitting .207! He wasn't the only player to have a candy bar named after him, but he was the one with the biggest mouth.

JETER, DEREK: Talk about pressure! Jeter was the rookie shortstop for the 1996 World Series winning Yankees, a team where most of the other players were already household names with million-dollar contracts. And the kid did real good! Jeter was the spark plug that kept the Yanks in the running all season long. Moreover, Jeter took the American League's Rookie of the Year Award as well as the World Series Trophy. (See also Phenom.)

> **? DID YOU KNOW**
>
> *That if you catch a ball at the park you can keep it? In the old days, before 1920, fans were required to return the ball to the umpire.*

Randy Johnson, the tallest man to ever play Major League Baseball.

DID YOU KNOW?

That a baseball has 116 stitches, the same number as beads on a rosary?

JOHNSON, RANDY: The Big Unit, as they call him in Seattle, is the tallest guy in baseball. In fact, the Seattle Mariners' ace is the tallest player ever to play Major League Baseball. If your team is playing Seattle, get tickets to see Johnson pitch. At 6 feet 10 inches, this giant southpaw isn't exactly Sean Connery, but he's got a fastball that's worth a second look.

JOURNEYMAN: A journeyman is a player who's been up in the majors for a while. He's probably seen his share of glory and disappointment and takes things in stride. He is a steadying influence on the younger players. Where do they get this stuff? For one thing, you'd think that a journeyman would be going somewhere, like on a journey. But he's not. He's already been there. And for another, he's probably the first one out of the cab at Baseball Annie's "dance hall."

JUICED BAT: A bat is said to be juiced, loaded, hollow, doctored, corked, or fiddled when it has been hollowed out and filled up with something else — like cork, or rubber, or fresh air. It's like filling up the cookie jar with "Dad's" and passing them off as mom's. And it doesn't work! Physics has determined that the juiced bat gives no advantage to a hitter at all: It may get him thrown out of the game, but it won't make a darned bit of difference to his batting average.

JUNK MAN: The junk man has been around the circuit for a while. He hasn't got much of a fastball anymore, but he's picked up a cartload of trashy pitches over the years, and he's still got something worth selling to the bull pen. You can expect a junk man to throw a lot of curve balls, sliders, and other off speed pitches, but you won't see him at the neighborhood garage sales.

K: You've probably seen people hanging them over the fences during a pitchers' duel. The K stands for strikeout. They have trouble spelling in baseball. When the number of Ks looped over the fence approaches 10, you better hope the pitcher is on *your* team's starting rotation. (See also Strikeout.)

KNUCKLEBALL: Pitchers who throw these are dan-

DID YOU KNOW?

That the first commissioner of baseball was named after the mountain that his father fought for in the Civil War? Judge Kenesaw Mountain Landis (below) was appointed to the office of commissioner in 1920, where his first responsibility was to clean up the Black Sox Scandal of 1919.

gerous. I mean it. They may not look like much, but just watch those strapping great hitters go down swinging one after the other. With hardly any windup, and a very peculiar grip on the ball, the knuckleball floats toward the plate looking for all the world like a drunk Junebug. Knuckleballers definitely look like knuckleheads, but the last laugh is on us; they can flutter those things in all day long without wearing out their arms.

LARKIN, BARRY: The National League MVP for 1995, Larkin was the first shortstop to hit 30 home runs and steal 30 bases in the same year. He's fast, he's as agile as a cat, and he's so smooth they call him "Silk" around the clubhouse. Larkin is what you call a hometown hero. He was born and raised in Cincinnati, where he holds the regular job at shortstop.

LARUSSA, TONY: Tony LaRussa is living proof that you don't have to be dumb to understand baseball. He was a good player, but he wasn't good enough to play very long in the Bigs. So he played in the minors, where he studied baseball and law. When he graduated from law school, he also graduated from Bush League baseball and was hired on to manage the White Sox. And he learned real good. If anybody is counting, he's won Manager of the Year Awards in three different cities. Here's a tip: There have been five baseball managers who graduated from law school. Four of them are in the Hall of Fame, and the other one is Tony LaRussa. If I were a betting girl...

LEADOFF BATTER: This guy is number one on the hit parade for very good reasons. He isn't the team's best batter, but he is probably the leader in on base percentage (which means that he gets on base more often than anybody else on the team). He probably draws a lot of walks, can run like the wind, and has no problem standing in to "take one for the team." (See also Hit by the Pitch.) The strategy is to get him on base for the cleanup hitters and to get him to bat more often.

LEATHERMAN: A team player who is known as a "leatherman" isn't kinky, it means he's better with his hands than he is with the bat. So he's not a total loser.

LEE, BILL: Bill Lee wasn't the greatest pitcher to play in modern baseball, but he was one of the strangest. When he was picked to pitch game seven of the 1975 World Series for Boston, Cincinnati manager Sparky Anderson told the press: "I don't know who's gonna win this game, but my pitcher's goin' into the Hall of Fame."

A-Z

Diamonds are a girls BEST FRIEND

LIZZIE MURPHY

Lizzie "Spike" Murphy played the game of baseball with intensity worthy of the nic-name both on the field, and off. As a youngster, playing for a semi-pro team, she was offered $5 a game plus a share of the take. The 'take' was collected by passing a hat among the crowd. This is probably the origin of the word 'cheap seats'. When the word got out that the team's hot new first baseman was a woman, the cheap seats became a valued commodity. But the team went back on it's deal, offering Murphy a meager share of the increased profits. When the bus was ready to roll for the next stop on the barn storming tour, Murphy refused to board the bus without her proper share of the loot. For Murphy, fairness and equality was the law. Eventually, as the story goes, the manager saw things her way, and Murphy headed down the road to future glory with heavy pockets and a berth in baseball history. Murphy wasn't in the game purely for the money, but she made a fair amount of it. In her many years with the semi-pro All Stars of Boston, Lizzy supplemented her salary as a first baseman with baseball cards, which she had printed up and sold at the stadium sidelines. On a good day, Murphy was known to sell fifty bucks worth.

Spaceman Bill Lee read the quote and responded: "I don't know who's gonna win this game either, but when it's over, I'm goin' to the Hall of Foam!" As good as his word, Lee and the Red Sox drowned their sorrow in a local pub while the Reds took home the trophy.

LEFTY: They say lefties are clumsy; that they're forever breaking dishes and spilling drinks. But left-handed pitchers can fool you. Half the time they're flakey, the other half they're too clever by a long shot, and you *never* know where their hands are going. In baseball, if a guy can throw the ball in the direction of home plate with his left hand, you can be sure he makes enough money to pay for all the broken china.

LINE DRIVE: You wouldn't expect a line drive to have people running around in circles would you? Well it does. We tried to use a line to teach my sister to drive, and she's still going in circles. Also known as a liner, clothesline, and frozen rope, the line drive is a well hit ball which has little chance of leaving the park, but a very good chance of getting a batter into the loop.

LONG BALL: There is nothing more glorious than a long ball at twilight. It's a wonderful thing to watch. The guy who does it is smiling and trotting around the bases, all proud of himself. No wonder he's proud, he just hit a home run!

LONG MAN: Get your mind out of the gutter, girls. Baseball players are the same as everybody else. In metric or imperial. The long man is a pitcher who doesn't start the game, doesn't finish it, but does

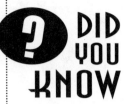

DID YOU KNOW

That in 1977 the Dodgers became the first team to have four players with 30 or more home runs in a season? They were Steve Garvey, Ron Saye, Dusty Baker and Reggie Smith. I guess you might call them the artful Dodgers.

the job in-between. He's also known as the long reliever.

MADDUX, GREG: Maddux is currently regarded as the greatest pitcher in the game. His pitching numbers are fantastic, but more than that, he's a great guy to watch in the field. Maddux flags down infield hits that most pitchers would let bounce out behind second base. Watch for Maddux to be playing on championship contenders. If Maddux is in your team's rotation, you can be sure they're a contender.

MANTLE, MICKEY: The 1950s were a Mickey decade. Everybody who was anybody was named Mickey. Mickey Mantle, Mickey Rooney, Mickey Mouse. They were everywhere! The one we're interested in is Mickey Mantle. Mr. Baseball. Mantle was the handsomest of the three, and the one that was best at playing baseball. And he was probably the most popular in his day. He won the Triple Crown (batting average, home runs, RBIs), won all the batting titles, and signed autographs. In the 1950s baseball was everything, and Mickey Mantle was baseball.

MAYS, WILLIE: If there was any justice in the universe, this guy should have been born Willie

Octobers. In May, he was just getting started. He was a sandlot hero who made it to the big time, but he was never too big to have time for the kids on the sandlots. And New York loved him. When Willie Mays and the Giants left New York for the west coast in 1958, nobody was sure which they would miss most, Willie or the Giants. And Willie missed New Yorkers, too. He felt unappreciated on the Golden Coast. And since nobody named a candy bar after him in California, he came back to Gotham City with the Mets in '72. He was still good, and New York still loved him but he was no Willie Mays.

McLAIN, DENNY: You won't read too much about Denny McLain in the baseball books. He may have been the last pitcher to win more than 30 games, but after leaving the Detroit Tigers he fell from grace. Badly. In 1968 he won 31 games with a 1.96 ERA and led the Tigers to the World Series Championship. By the mid-1970s he had gained more than 100 pounds, been imprisoned for cocaine-related charges, and worse, wound up selling organs at a local Detroit music store. McLain is quoted as saying, "When you win out there between the white lines, you can live any way you want." Unfortunately for McLain, this didn't include snorting the white lines.

MEAL TICKET: Remember that schmo with the deep pockets you dumped last year? The meal ticket? The guy who you could always count on for a last-minute date? Baseball has them too. They may not be much on the field, but you can count on them for a free lunch, or a hit, when the chips are down.

That a baseball weighs the same as a hockey puck?

DID YOU KNOW

That many athletes who conquer one sport often try to make the grade in others? In 1994 Michael Jordan signed with the Birmingham Barrons baseball club. Millionaire Michael Jordan bought the team a new bus, but his skills on the diamond weren't as deep as his pockets. At the end of the season he packed it up and went back to being the greatest basketball player of all time!

MENDOZA LINE: The Mendoza Line could be one of three things: (1) a place you will not find on any map, no matter how far south you go; (2) the question nobody knows in Trivial Pursuit; or (3) a batting average of .200. The answer is all three, but mostly number 3. When a batter is said to be flirting with the Mendoza Line, his batting average is around .200. This would not be a good time to renegotiate a long-term contract.

MERKLE, FRED: Fred Merkle is famous for his boner. Really. Merkle's boner happened in 1908, and everybody at New York's Polo Grounds was watching. It was the ninth inning, Merkle was on first, somebody else was on third, and there were two out. The batter smacked the ball out between first and second base and the runner went home. Game over, right? Wrong. Merkle heads for the clubhouse, and the shortstop touches second base with the ball. Merkle is out, the run doesn't count. In the end, it cost the Giants the championship and Merkle his reputation.

MIDSUMMER CLASSIC: This midsummer night's dream is hardly much ado about nothing. You might not see King Lear, but the dukes of the dugout are all on hand. And though they're hardly competition for the Bard, all the baseball scribes are pulling out the stops to bring colorful copy to the next day's newsstands. The Midsummer Classic is the All-Star Game.

MINORS: Being of legal age is certainly no guarantee that you won't be treated like a minor if you don't hit the ball. They don't care how old you are.

Ladies DAY

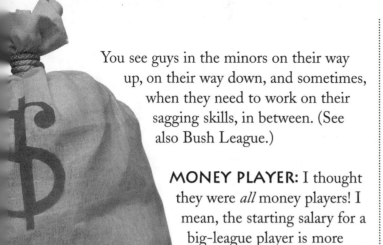

You see guys in the minors on their way up, on their way down, and sometimes, when they need to work on their sagging skills, in between. (See also Bush League.)

MONEY PLAYER: I thought they were *all* money players! I mean, the starting salary for a big-league player is more money than I'll ever see at one time. They don't do all this hitting and running for the love of the game. A money player is a guy who earns his salary when the going gets tough. (See also Clutch Player.)

Albert Belle has never even seen the Mendoza Line.

MOP UP MAN: It's hard to believe that these high paid pros have chores to do, but it's true. Even pitchers have to clean up after a bad game. When the team is down 17-1, and the starting pitcher is crying in the showers, they send out a guy called the mop up man to try to salvage some respect for his failing teammates. It ain't a glamorous job, but somebody's got to do it. If they hired women in baseball, they'd probably give them this assignment, but since they don't, they send out an over-the-hill hurler to do the dirty work.

MUD: My laundry room is littered with boxes claiming "secret ingredients" to get

Diamonds are a girls BEST FRIEND

LIZZY MURPHY: PART II

Lizzy Murphy doesn't have a line in the Major League record book, but if you look hard enough, you can see the smudge she left. The Queen of Baseball, as she was known, held a regular job at first base for some of the best minor league teams in the eastern loop between 1918 and 1935. The men she played with were mostly guys on their way up to the Big Club, and guys on their way down. But there wasn't a minor league team in the east who wouldn't have wanted her on the line up card. And it wasn't for her good looks. It was because she was a good ball player. She was as steady and effective an infielder as any man of her day. And don't forget that in her day, women couldn't even vote! But she was as good as any of the men, and better than most. Which is what brings us back to the record book. In 1922, Lizzie was chosen to represent the American League and their New England farm clubs in an all star game against the Boston Red Sox. So she became the first woman ever to play in a Major League All Star game. Six years later, in 1928, she represented the National League in an all star game against the Braves, making her the first person, man or woman, to ever play for both the American and National League all star teams. So next time somebody tells you that women couldn't cut it in today's tough Major League world, tell them to look up Lizzy Murphy.

dirt, grime, and mud out of clothes. The mud we're talking about has secret ingredients to fight back. Since early in the century, pro baseballs have been rubbed up with Lena Blackburn's concoction of Delaware mud and a host of secret ingredients to dull the slick surface of new baseballs. Before each game, the umpire rubs 60 balls with this stuff. In the old days, fans who caught a ball were required to throw it back. Today, they know that people figure they have a right to any ball going into the crowds, so they rub up enough to get them through the game.

NATIONAL LEAGUE: The National League is known as the "Senior Circuit" because it was formed by crusty old men in 1877, a few years before the "Junior Circuit," the American League. From that day on, the owners of the teams have been in charge. The players are just employees who do what they're told. The chief distinction between the AL and the NL is that the NL is a "fastball game." The pitchers favor the fastball over the fancy stuff.

NIGHTCAP: If a baseball fan ever asks you out for a nightcap, say no. Unless you're up for a doubleheader. When a previous game has been rained out or otherwise uncompleted, doubleheaders are scheduled to make up the game. The nightcap is the second game. (See also, Double Header.)

NO-HITTER: The no-hitter is the sine qua non of pitching. In a no-hitter, the pitcher tosses a complete game without giving up a legitimate hit. It is possible, however, for a pitcher to throw a no-hitter and still lose the game: If a batter reaches base on

DID YOU KNOW

That early players wore a glove on each hand? Many players wore kid leather gloves with the fingers cut off to make handling the balls easier.

DID YOU KNOW

That the New York Yankees were the first team to have numbers on their uniforms? In 1929, the numbers on their jerseys corresponded to their spot in the batting order.

an error, or a walk, and comes around to score the winning run, the pitcher will go down as tossing a no-hit game, but the box score will record a loss.

NOMO, HIDEO: Nomo is the only Japanese pitcher in Major League baseball, so you can't miss him. He wasn't the first Japanese pitcher to get to the Bigs, however. That honor goes to Masanori Murakami, who went 5-1 for San Francisco in the early 1960's. If your team is playing the Dodgers, go watch Nomo pitch. His delivery looks more like an ancient religious ritual than a windup; but whatever he's doing works, since hardly anybody hits him!

OFFENSIVE: The guys who sit behind me and Julia at the ballpark are offensive. They catcall the players, the umpires, the manager, and Julia. *On* the diamond, the team that is batting is known as the offensive team (and it's not because they all spit when they come to bat), while the team on the field is the defensive team. Both teams get equal opportunities to be offensive. So last August I took my opportunity to be offensive and spilled beer on the guys behind us!

OFFICIAL SCORER: The official scorer is not the team leader for most entries in his little black book. In fact, he (or she) is the off-field official charged with deciding what happened after a play is over. The scorer decides, among other things, when a fielder is to be charged with an error or whether a pitch which gets past the catcher is a "passed ball" or a "wild pitch." If you've ever wondered why a blundering third baseman or defeated shortstop is looking high into the stands after a bad play, it's not that he's appealing to the gods for a chance to do it over; he isn't doing silent penance; he's hoping the ball was deemed "unplayable" to keep the charge of "error" from his personal record book.

ON DECK: Ahoy, matey, this sailor is the next batter to come to the plate. The "man on deck" can be seen swinging bats off to the side of home plate in a designated area called the "on deck circle."

ONE GAME AT A TIME: This is how ball players always respond when asked almost any question: "I'm gonna play it one game at a time." So what are the other options here? "I'm gonna play all the games at once" or "I thought I'd play the first few real good, then dry up for a while"? What he's *thinking* is "If I don't start hittin' the thang, real good like, then I'll be ridin' buses in North Dakota again." But what he's *saying* is "I just try to do my job and play it one game at a time." Some of these fellas ought to take some of their hard-earned cash and buy themselves a public relations consultant.

PAIGE, SATCHEL: Leroy Satchel Paige may have been the greatest pitcher to ever pull on a uniform, but don't bother looking him up in the record books. Most of his career was played in the Negro Leagues where the records didn't count. By the time the "color barrier" was broken in 1947, Paige was past his prime but still good enough to play in the major leagues. (See also Cy Young Award.)

PAYOFF PITCH: I know this sounds like somebody's making money under the table, but actually, it just means strike three.

Satchell Paige, reaching back for a little something extra.

PEGGY LEE FASTBALL: Norma Dolorous Egstrom, AKA Miss Peggy Lee, was a very sexy crooner with a charming mole on her face and more hits to her credit than many successful major-leaguers. It was her greatest hit, however, that immortalized her name at the ballpark. Those halfhearted fastballs with more form than speed are known as Peggy Lee fastballs. Is that all there is?

PERFECT GAME: In the perfect game, you give 27 guys a chance to score, and nobody even gets to first base. And it can give you a reputation. A girl I went to high school with did this sort of thing, and she was called names I won't repeat in public. If a pitcher does this regularly, they call him the "Cy Young winner." It's definitely a man's world.

PHENOM: The true phenom is about as common as the perfect mother-in-law. You hear a lot about them in the early going, but once the bloom is off the rose and the rolls of Martha Stewart wallpaper start to arrive, you hear less about their good deeds and more about their omissions. For a top-ranked rookie, being touted as a phenom often means an unspeakable signing bonus, a short visit to the minor-league club, and a sudden run-in with the reality of Major League Baseball. The phenom with the 108 mph fastball, the .400 hitter, and the unstoppable base thief will more likely go up in flames than down in history.

PIAZZA, MIKE: I like mine with green olives and basil. But I like Mike Piazza no matter what he's wearing. Mostly, he wears the catcher's gear for Los Angeles and delivers to second base as fast as anybody in the business. But he can deliver a spicy meatball from the batter's box, too. If there's anything anywhere near the plate, he's not gonna eat it in the park, he's gonna take it home.

PICK-OFF: This is the same thing in baseball as it is everywhere else. Specifically, the pitcher, or the catcher, tries to pick-off the base runner. If the runner strays a little too far from the bag, he just might get sacked in the pick-off. (See also Hold the Runner.)

> **? DID YOU KNOW**
>
> *That the spitball was invented by George Hildebrand in 1902? In his day, the pitch was legal! The spitball was not banned until 1920, although any player throwing it before the ban was allowed to use it until they retired. The last man to legally throw the spitball was Burleigh Grimes, who retired in 1934. Today, hardly anybody throws the spitball. They use K. Y. Jelly instead.*

A-Z

Diamonds are a girls BEST FRIEND

Isabel Alvarez

In 1947 the first Cuban woman to play baseball in the United States, Eulalia Gonzales, was signed to the Racine Belles. But her American dream was short-lived when she developed a bad case of homesickness and returned to Cuba. Following in her footsteps was Isabel Alvarez, who arrived in 1949, with a little stronger stomach and a driving passion to play, *Pelota De Baseball.*

Alvarez's talents were developed in the Cuban women's league, Estrellas Cubanas, which was made up of the best female players Cuba had to offer. A budding talent, Alvarez, who was born in 1933, made the team at the tender age of 12. By 15 she was chomping at the bit for a chance to try out for the AAGBL, and the southpaw pitcher won a spot on the Chicago Colleens. She remained there for two seasons, until the owners dropped the idea of a women's farmteam. Quicker than you can say "no money honey," the women were let go.

Fortunately, Alvarez was soon pushing up daisies, for the Fort Wayne Daisies that is, a higher ranking division of the AAGBL. Speaking very little English, she found herself feeling very alone and segregated from the other players. But she stuck it out and wrapped up her baseball career as a member of the AAGBL. Today she is proud to be part of a select group of women who got a chance to make history, playing the Grand Old Game.

PINCH RUNNER: I don't know if this has ever happened to you, but when it happened to me, I'd have sent the guy sprawling on his keester if he hadn't already been running. The pinch probably left a bruise, but I couldn't quite see it. On the diamond, like on the dance floor, the pinch runner is usually a move of desperation. You're down a run or two, it's late, and the only guy to get to base has legs like a farmer. He may be great in the field and good with blunt instruments, but when it comes to stealing, he's got two left feet. Which is where the pinch runner comes in. The manager looks along the bench for some youngster with long legs and sends him in to run for the sluggish slugger. The hitter is now out of the game for good, but the team pins its hopes on the incoming pinch runner to make it home.

PINE TAR: You'd never get this stuff off your floors. Pine tar is that gooey stuff you see dripping down the trees when you go camping. If you've ever touched it, you know that it's sticky, smelly stuff that is hell to wash out. Ball players rub this stuff all over themselves. It's not that they're all woodsy types who like to smell like real men; they smear it on their bats to give them a better grip. Then they rub their hands on their pants, shirts, faces, and arms. It's fine for these guys to have a better grip on the bat, but it's hell in the laundry room!

Every day is Ladies Day

? DID YOU KNOW

That Jeremiah Denny was the last man to play barehanded? He left the game, in 1894, due to calluses.

97
A-Z

PITCHER: The pitcher's job is to prevent the batter from hitting the ball. There are more names for the pitcher than any living human being ought to know. Some generic names are: hurler, flipper, pivot, arm, front end, right-hander, left-hander, submarine, butterfly, sidearm, knuckleballer, fireman, middleman, reliever, long man, short man, junk man, setup man, closer, stopper, ace. We've probably missed your favorites, but you probably already know more than is good for you.

PITCHER'S RUBBER: This isn't something the pitcher keeps in his back pocket for after the game, and it's a good thing, too. He stands on it. In his spiked shoes! It's 24 inches long, six inches wide, and he *must* keep his foot on it when he pitches.

PITCHOUT: This is a nasty bit of work, and it fails more often than it works. The runner on base is wandering a little too far off the base, and it looks like the steal sign is on. The catcher calls for the "pitchout": The pitcher will deliver a strike well out of the batter's reach, and the catcher is standing up and waiting for it. By the time the runner knows what is happening, the catcher has thrown the ball to second base, catching the base thief red-handed.

PIVOT: Watch the play when there is a man on first and the ball is hit to the left side of the field. The second baseman goes to his base, catches the toss, pivots, and throws to first for the double play. This is why they call the second baseman the pivot.

PLATOONING: Baseball isn't that different from life. Sofi, a lawyer I know, has got two good men vying for the every-night assignment. "Some of us should be so lucky!" I told her. So she sees her botanist one week and the prosecutor the next, and she's just takin' her time. No commitments. She says she'd rather wait and see how they do once the bloom is off the rose. It's the same for a baseball manager. He might have two third basemen, and, finding neither of them too exciting, he might decide not to decide. As a result, one player will get the nod one game, and the other guy will get the nod the next. If one of these guys starts batting .300, the other guy better pack his suitcase.

PLAYER TO BE NAMED LATER: You'd think that by the time they're old enough to play baseball, they'd have a name, wouldn't you? Well they do, but in the baseball sweepstakes, there's a lot of weird language. When a team trades a player, they trade for all sorts of things: players, money, considerations, and players to be named later. How would *you* like to be the player to be named later?

POP FLY: I found one of these once at a ball game. I didn't hear him buzzing in my cup until the third inning. Disgusting. They were hitting a lot of them out on the field, too. A pop fly is a high fly ball that doesn't make it to the outfield.

POWER ALLEY: This sounds like the place a group of women might wait to ambush the guy in the office who insists on calling them "honey." On the ball field, the power alley is to the right or left of dead center in the outfield. (See also Gap; The Hole.)

PULL THE BALL: Nevermind any smart remarks here. Baseball is a ball game. You hit the ball, throw the ball, catch the ball, spit on the ball, roll

> **? DID YOU KNOW**
>
> *That good eyesight is as important to a batter as strong arms? Here are four secrets to what happens when the bat meets the ball: (1) hitting the top of the ball will result in a ground ball; (2) hitting the middle will give you a line drive; (3) hitting the bottom of the ball will get you a fly ball; and (4) hitting the underside of the ball will send the ball into the stands behind the batter's box.*

DID YOU KNOW

That in 1901 Cy Young won 33 games, the most ever by a modern-day pitcher? His career record shows 511 wins, the most ever, and 313 losses, the most ever. So they named the award for the year's greatest pitcher after him. But the story doesn't end there. Satchel Paige, whose career is not recorded because he played in the Negro Leagues, is believed to have won 2,000 games in his career; more games than Young's wins and losses combined. Of those 2,000 wins, 250 were shutouts and 45 were no-hitters. So go figure why they named the award after Cy Young!

the ball, but *pull* the ball? Pulling the ball is what the great hitters in the game are said to be able to do, though to watch them, it just looks like they are hitting it. The batter is able to control the moment of contact between the bat and the ball in such a way as to force the ball into the field opposite from the "hand" from which he is hitting. That is, a right-handed batter will "pull" the ball into left field; the left-handed batter will "pull" the ball into right field. Pulling the ball is not like an "early swing," although the early swing will still have the same general effect — without the power of the "pulled ball." Physicists are in as much disagreement with the mechanics of pulled balls as they are with crop circles.

QUICK PITCH: A quick pitch is illegal. And it ought to be. This really happened: Returning to New York from Italy, our plane picked up some passengers from Germany. A guy who looked like a cross between Rudolf Nureyev and Arnold Schwarzenegger stood next to me in the luggage pickup line. He lifted his bag from the carousel, turned to face me, his pale blue eyes shining deep into my surprised peepers, and said, "If you come with me to the Plaza, I will make your stay in New York ecstasy." Just like that. No "Hello my name is Prince Sigfried, "no "Can we share a cab?" Just straight to the point. Quick pitch. It's like that in baseball, too. The pitcher has to give the base runner all the right signals before he can make an offering to the batter. If Count Handsome had gone through the established rituals, I might not be talking about this in public, but as it happened, I gave him a look that might have killed some men and he strutted away. If the pitcher doesn't come to a full stop before

Diamonds are a girls BEST FRIEND

Margaret Nabel

Margaret Nabel had baseball in her blood. She came from Staten Island, where it was said there was four baseball teams per square mile. In 1914, the year she graduated from high school, Nabel joined up with the New York Bloomer Girls, the premier women's baseball club in the east. Her powerful arm was matched only by her ambition to own and operate a baseball club. By 1920, she had wrestled control of the team from it's owners, and took over the organization lock, stock and barrel. For the next 23 years, Nabel and the New York Bloomer Girls barnstormed up and down the coast, taking on all challengers from Nova Scotia to Florida, and winning enough of the games to make the operation profitable. It was difficult to meet the team payroll from gate receipts, so Nabel sold postcards of her team, game schedules and gave controversial interviews to anybody who would buy them. Her ability to promote the team was unsurpassed among Bloomer Girl teams, allowing her to get away with calling her team 'The Female Champions of The World'. By the early 1930's, the Bloomer Girls era was drawing to a close. A new sport had been invented, and deemed more suitable for women. The game was softball, and Nabel would have none of it. Rather than find herself the pilot of a team of softies, she disbanded the franchise in 1933 and opened up a candy store back on Staten Island.

throwing to the plate, the umpire will call a balk, and the runners will strut up to the next base.

RANGE: A baseball player is said to have range when he really *can* be in two places at once. Their range is determined by how much of the field they can play and get away with. Getting caught short in the outfield might just allow somebody to get home on the range.

RBI: Also known as a "ribbie," this is something that Adam got one more of than Eve. It's also one of the things that counts most in baseball. An RBI is a run batted in. If a batter puts the ball into play and a run scores, he is awarded an RBI. If he hits a home run, he gets RBIs for each runner and for himself. In baseball, like in the Bible, having more ribbies than anybody else gives you major bragging rights.

RED LIGHT: We hate to give Baseball Annie so much ink, but we want to make it clear that when a ball player gets a red light, it's not what she hangs up in her boudoir window. A red light is a signal from the third base coach to the batter. The boss wants you to "take" the pitch. For reasons of his own, the manager does not want the batter to swing at the ball. A batter who takes a poke on a red light

Cal Ripkin

may very well find himself on the bench, or at least on the receiving end of a tongue lashing.

RESERVE CLAUSE: No relation to Santa Claus, all baseball players hated the reserve clause. It was worse than a shotgun wedding. Once a player signed a contract with a team, he became their property, and they reserved the right to sell him, trade him, send him to the minors, or send him packing. The player, on the other hand, had the right to do as he was told and not complain about it. He could not negotiate with any other team under any circumstances. Before free agency came into being in 1976, this arrangement was a life sentence. Divorce was unheard of. Today, once a player's contract with a team has ended, and he's been through waivers, anybody can legally court him. (See also Free Agent; Waivers.)

RESIN BAG: The resin bag is part of every pitcher's standard equipment. You can find this handy little package of dried up, powdered pine tar sitting out on the field behind the pitcher's mound, ready for him to pick up and dust over his throwing hand. It makes his hand sticky. Why does he want sticky fingers? Who knows? It's a guy thing. (See also Pine Tar.)

RIPKIN, CAL: Julia says Cal Ripkin reminds her of the guy who sat at the front of the class in grade 11 chemistry. You never paid much attention to him, but he was always there. I mean, it seems like the guy hasn't missed a day's work since Babe Ruth retired. In fact, in 1996 he broke Lou Gehrig's record for most consecutive games played. He does fabulous work, makes tons of money, and makes it all look so easy!

DID YOU KNOW

That in the old days, the Boston Red Sox used to win the World Series? Before 1920, they won five of them. Then they sold Babe Ruth to New York and haven't won since. Go figure. Sounds like a curse to me.

ROAD TRIP: This is like Bing and Bob leaving town without Dorothy Lamour. And though they stay in five-star hotels, it ain't Shangri-la. A road trip generally consists of a series of games in "away" parks. They might play three games in New York, spend "get-away day" on a flight to California, play three or four games on the coast, and head back after the last game to get ready for a "home stand." Calling this a road trip is a bit misleading: Nobody in the big leagues would be caught dead on a bus!

RODRIGUEZ, IVAN: I told my friend Gail that Rodriguez had the best arm in all of baseball, and she agreed, but she said he only had the second-best tush in the American League. Brady Anderson got her vote for the best buns. But Rodriguez isn't just another pretty catcher; his quick moves make guys like Brady Anderson think twice about stealing second.

Pete Rose, AKA Charlie Hustle. "Who me?"

ROLE PLAYERS: This is what Baseball Annie and her friends would like to do after the game. But that's not what the radio announcer is talking about. He's talking about the roles that the players like to play: the bat man, who specializes in hitting; the thief, who swipes bases; the ice man, who comes in to pitch the final innings. You will see these guys on the bench and in the bull pen, and you'll see them at Baseball Annie's Dance Hall and Emporium.

ROOKIE: If this was chess, the rookie would be the guy on the ends. In baseball, it means the guy who tries the hardest because it's his first year playing. (See also Phenom.)

ROSE, PETE: Depending on your point of view, Pete Rose is either one of the greatest players of modern days, or a stinker. Nicknamed "Charlie Hustle," Rose played harder than any kid in the park for nearly 25 years. He is the career leader in hits, singles, at bats, and games played, but you won't see his name in Cooperstown. Following his long and glorious career, Rose was accused of being in serious trouble with gamblers and was banned from the game for life.

ROSTER: The manager's little black book of who's available tonight. He has 25 able-bodied men he can call on (don't you wish?) to fill the "lineup card" for a game. This includes pitchers, bench-warmers, and designated hitters.

ROTATION: Every team has four or five pitchers who can start a game. They take turns doing this, which is why they call it a rotation. Knowing the

DID YOU KNOW

That baseball big shot Branch Rickey became a farmer in 1919? In that year he established the farm system. Major-league teams would own and operate minor-league franchises where they would cultivate players for the big leagues.

DID YOU KNOW?

That one of the greatest players in baseball was a man who belonged in prison, not in the dugout? Ty Cobb, the Georgia Peach, is reputed to have assaulted so many people on and off the field, that you could nearly fill a stadium with his victims. He carried a Luger with him wherever he went, along with a brown bag containing more than a million dollars.

names of the pitchers in your starting team's rotation is very important if you want to look like a knowledgeable fan.

RUNNER'S INTERFERENCE: What do you think happens to a runner if he gets hit by the ball? I mean aside from being carted off in an ambulance? You won't believe it. He's out. I don't mean he's out cold, I mean he's out. If, in the opinion of the umpires, the runner should have been able to avoid a thrown ball, they call him out. And that might sound unfair, but listen. When the game was first invented, the players threw the ball at the runner on purpose! Hitting the runner with the ball wasn't an accident, or interference, it was how you got him out. They changed it when nobody wanted to get to first base. How would you like it if somebody was throwing a baseball at your head every time you got on base?

RUTH, BABE: I don't need to tell you about Babe Ruth. Everybody knows everything about Babe Ruth. Where I come from, knowing about Babe Ruth is right up there with knowing the Pledge of Allegiance.

SABR: These are a group of grown men who spend their leisure time analyzing the most esoteric and trivial statistics and stories of the game. They have magazines, T-shirts, and conferences. So who'd want to be saddled with a guy who's always rehashing last year's performance? AKA: The Society for American Baseball Research

SACRIFICE: I know what you're thinking. What do men know about sacrifice? When there are less than

No, this is not John Goodman, this is the real Babe Ruth.

two out, and a team has a base runner, they will often sacrifice the batter to move the runner ahead. The sacrifice fly is hit as far away from the base runner as possible so that he can tag up and get into scoring position. The sacrifice bunt is an infield play that draws the infielders away from their bases, allowing the runner to advance. The baseball gods reward sacrifice, too: A sacrifice does not count against the batter in calculating his average!

The girls of summer.

SAFETY SQUEEZE PLAY: Sounds like a contradiction in terms, doesn't it? In the safety squeeze, the runner on third makes sure that the pitch is actually hit on the ground before hightailing it for home plate. It's like making sure your roommate is still up before inviting your date in for a drink. (See also Squeeze Play; Suicide Squeeze Play.)

SANDLOT: The sandlot is what real men call the baseball stadium. I mean for heaven's sake, the thing probably cost $100 million to build, and they call it a sandlot? These are the same guys who leave all their junk on the floor when they leave. I mean, really. They ought to call it the dump the way they treat it!

SCORING: You might think knowing the score is a cinch. But listen, there's more to scoring than knowing who's on top when it's over. Who did what to whom, how many times, and how many relievers were used is just as important. That's what the enthusiasts behind you at the ball game are doing bent over clipboards. They're scoring. Really.

SCHOTT, MARG: Marg Schott is a largely misunderstood person. I'm sure of it. Men don't understand women like Marg Schott. Neither do I, but at least I understand that I don't understand her. That may be the chief difference between women and men. At least when we don't know something, we know it. The colorful Schott owns the Cincinnati Reds, and she complains that she can't even smoke in her own private box. Do you feel sorry for her? Neither do I, but they make great hay in the tabloids about The Red Menace. So she's eccentric. So what, exactly, does eccentric mean when you're talking about people who have enough money to own sports franchises?

SCORING POSITION: Why does every red-blooded ball player want to get to first base? So that they can get into scoring position, of course. For these guys, scoring is everything, and they will do anything to get into position to do it. If you can beg, borrow, or steal a trip to second base, you're in scoring position. Now you may think that second base is a long way from home, but the runner is already halfway there. It's easier to score once you've been at the hot corner for a while, but on a good play you can do it from second.

SCOUTS: Believe me, there are no Boy Scouts in Major League Baseball. But a bunch of high-testosterone millionaires jetting around the country for eight months of the year are bound to be involved in the occasional jamboree. Bill Lee once said that it was not true that all major-league players "strayed" while on the road. He said there was a left fielder, once, for the Yankees who was never, ever known to have cheated on his wife. So scouts and scouting have nothing to do with good deeds and tying knots. Major-league scouts are guys who hang around baseball diamonds looking for men with potential. Sound familiar? All big-league teams have a staff of retired players and officials who comb the minor leagues looking for promising young men who need professional grooming. When I was growing up, this is what aunts were for.

SCREWBALL: There's a lot of screwballs in the game. There was Rube Waddell, the screwball pitcher who was always so late for the game that he got dressed on the field and did somersaults when he struck out a batter. Bill "Spaceman" Lee — the pitcher who said he put marijuana on his peanut butter sandwiches every morning — could be described as a screwball. And the word could easily be used to describe several team owners.

DID YOU KNOW

That the first All-Star Game was played in Chicago's Comiskey Park in 1933? The first home run was hit by the Sultan of Swat, Babe Ruth.

Diamonds are a girls BEST FRIEND

EDITH HOUGHTON

Edith 'The Kid' Houghton grew up in Philadelphia in the early 1900's. The City of Brotherly Love was a hotbed of baseball, and Houghton found herself in good company. Aside from having franchises in both the National and American leagues, Philadelphia was the home of one of the best Bloomer Girl teams of the time, the Philadelphia Bobbies. The name came not for their arresting talent, but from their pert hairdos. The Bobbies were managed by one of the best women in the business, Mary O'Gara. When Houghton showed up for try outs on the women's team, she was ten years old. She may have been only ten years old, but she wasn't exactly new to baseball. Since the age of six, Edith had been something of a local sensation, and the mascot of the local police team. As the team's mascot, she had a reserved seat at the games: She sat next to the Mayor of Philadelphia. Edith played with the Bobbies for the next several years, even touring Japan in an ill-fated barnstorm of the far east. But she outgrew the Bobbies and joined up with Margaret Nabel's New York Bloomer Girls, where she played until the team was disbanded in 1933. With no place to play real baseball, Edith resigned herself to playing softball until finally, she found a more suitable place for herself in the 'men's game'. In 1946, Edith Houghton became the first Major League scout, traveling around the country looking for talent for the Philadelphia Phillies.

When you hear about a screwball, however, it's usually a curve ball that curves the wrong way. (A right-hander's curve ball curves to the left, his screwball curves to the right.)

SEASON: It's not spicy, but it's often hot. And it goes on for a while. A baseball season is 162 games long; if it doesn't provide some variety, it'll get pretty boring for fans in the bleachers.

SEVENTH INNING STRETCH: Between the top and the bottom of the seventh inning, tradition has it that fans will rise from their seats and stretch. There are several theories behind the origins of this tradition: (1) The numb bum syndrome: Bums and bleachers have not changed since baseball began. One's soft, the other is hard. And the soft one gets sore after five or six long innings of contact with the hard one; (2) The bleacher creature review: A chance to check out the numb bums in the front rows; and (3) Some American president did it a long time ago. The story goes that he stood up and everybody got up in respect. He probably just had a numb bum.

SHAKE OFF A SIGNAL: You've probably had to do this yourself. Some guy is coming on to you, and you don't want any of it. You shake your head, you say "No," you stamp your foot, you make hand signals, and eventually he will get the point. Unless he's brain dead. This is the same for pitchers. Only, for the pitcher, he eventually has to "go home" with the guy flashing the smiles and signals. The catcher flashes his fingers between his legs, and the pitcher coyly shakes his head "No." The catcher wiggles his fingers between his legs again, and the pitcher shakes him off once more. This goes on until the pitcher finally gets the signal that he wants. If it goes on for too long, somebody is liable to come in from the bench to tell the pitcher he's being too choosy. Thank god that in real life, we can just tell the guy to drop dead. (See also Adding and Subtracting.)

SHORTSTOP: Like those gas station stops on a long trip, the shortstop is hardly ever short. Take Honus Wagner, for example. At 6 feet 4 inches and 230 pounds, he was hardly what you'd call a little guy. And he was the best shortstop there ever was! The shortstop is responsible for stopping anything that travels between second and third base.

SHUT OUT: Been there? Done it? Well, it feels about the same in baseball. A shutout is a game in which one side has scored no runs. The losing team, who has been "shut out," heads to the showers with their egos hung low; the winning team, who "shut 'em out," grins and backslaps all the way to the postgame tavern. There are things more humiliating than being shut out, but not many.

SIGNALS: In real life, you probably spend a lot of time trying to pick them up from the strong, silent types. In baseball games you can't miss them. You know the guy standing beside third base wiping his hand across his chest and tipping his cap? He's not just hyperactive, he's telling the batter what to do. (See also Green Light; Take.) The catcher isn't quite as obvious with his signals. He wiggles his fingers between his legs to communicate with the pitcher. If a guy did that to me, I wouldn't just throw a baseball at him, I'd slap his face. (See also Adding and Subtracting.)

? DID YOU KNOW

That Marilyn Monroe's husband (one of them) was Joltin' Joe DiMaggio? DiMaggio was such a consistent hitter that in 1941 he began the greatest hitting streak in history. Before he was finished, Joe had gathered 91 hits in 56 consecutive games, a record nobody even flirts with.

SLEEPING RABBIT STEAL: We're not going to tell you what the sleeping rabbit steal is. This kind of information is like knowing the secret handshake, so we're gonna make you work for it. (See Delayed Double Steal.)

SLUGGING PERCENTAGE: Add the number of bases cleanly acquired (a home run equals four bases, a triple three, a double two, a single one) and divide by the number of at bats. This equals the slugging percentage. (15 bases in 25 at bats = .600; 11 bases in 15 at bats = .733.)

SLUMP: Chronic PMS at the plate. Yogi Berra, who you will hear more from later, said it best: "Slump? I ain't in no slump. I just ain't hitting."

SMITH, OZZIE: They called him the Wizard of Aahs. If you saw Ozzie Smith play, then you saw infielding at its best. When you weren't "oohing," you would be "aahing."

SMOLTZ, JOHN: The Atlanta Braves have three of the best starting pitchers in the game: Greg Maddux, Tom Glavine, and John Smoltz. Smoltz saves his best performances for the postseason, but he's worth seeing any time. (See also Ace; Money Player.)

SPALDING, ALBERT: You'll find the name Spalding popping up all over the ballpark. The balls, the bats, the gloves, the uniforms, the merchandising — it all says Spalding. So who was he? He was a good pitcher in the 1860s and 1870s, but mostly he was the guy who made baseball into a business.

DID YOU KNOW?

That in 1936 the first elections for the Hall of Fame were held? The five American heroes to be honored that first year were Ty Cobb, Honus Wagner, Babe Ruth, Christy Mathewson, and Walter Johnson.

SPIKES: I don't know about you, but I can hardly walk in them. I mean, we do what we have to, but when I first heard that these guys did all this in spikes, I couldn't believe it. I mean, I could maybe mince to first base in three-inch pumps, but hey. AKA: Cleats

Albert Spalding, who made baseball a business.

SPRING TRAINING: What do you do to beat the February blahs? Ball players do the same thing: They head south for some sun, fun, and a little workout. In the east, they call this the Grapefruit League, in the west, it's the Cactus League. Aside from toning up to look great in those stretch pants and shirtsleeves, ball players are working to earn their spots on the regular team. Many a veteran has had one too many Christmas dinners and been left behind in the Florida sunshine while some slim rookie goes north with the big club.

SQUEEZE PLAY: Getting a guy home sometimes involves a squeeze play. In the squeeze play, the runner on third runs on the pitch, and the batter bunts the ball in an attempt to create a distraction. I did this for my friend Julia a couple of times, leaving her with the hungry hunk while I made my excuses for an early night. (See also Safety Squeeze Play; Suicide Squeeze Play.)

No, Rickey Henderson is not lying down on the job, he's stealing third.

STAND-UP DOUBLE, TRIPLE: A stand-up hit is just about what it sounds like. The ball is hit sufficiently hard or placed so well that the batter gets to the base without having to slide. The folks in the laundry room particularly appreciate the stand-up hit.

STEAL: Baseball is one of the few games where crime pays. Sneaking around when nobody's looking can definitely win games in this sport. Watch the constant cat and mouse game between the pitcher and base runner. The runner is trying to get a head start toward second base while the pitcher "looks him back" closer to first. Once the pitcher has begun his delivery, the runner can go like hell before the catcher gets the ball and throws it. If he beats the ball to the base, he gets to stay there: a stolen base. If the ball gets there first and the runner is tagged, it's not a steal, it's an out.

STEINBRENNER, GEORGE: This is the guy who owns the New York Yankees. Most people believe that the team's owners should choose a management team then butt out. Steinbrenner doesn't. He is a control freak who refuses to lose.

STENGLE, CASEY: Baseball owes a debt to Casey Stengle. In fact, all of America owes a debt to Casey Stengle. He was the first man to perfect the art of talking a lot without saying anything. Sort of like the Bob Dylan of baseball. Stengle was a great player, a manager, and one of baseball's most colorful and often quoted contributors. The problem is, he didn't speak English. He spoke something they call "Stenglese." Speaking of his best pitcher, he

DID YOU KNOW

That the first declared free agent was a bottom feeder? It's true. Catfish Hunter was declared a free agent in 1975 and went to work at Yankee Stadium, after the Yankees won the bidding war for his services.

Diamonds are a girls BEST FRIEND

BERNICE GERA

"Play ball!" That's all Bernice Gera wanted to do. Throughout the 1960s she tried endlessly to get a job in baseball, but the boys' club was tightly locked. Then in 1967, Gera figured it out — she would become a baseball umpire!

Her road to a spot behind the plate was riddled with disappointment. She had to fight her way into umpiring school; after countless rejections, she was accepted by Jim Finlay's Florida Baseball Umpire School. Upon graduation, in 1969, she returned home to Queens and gained experience officiating high-school and semipro games. She then applied to dozens of minor-league organizations. After obtaining legal counsel Gera was finally awarded a contract with the New York-Penn League in 1969. But, the celebrations were premature; the head of the league voided her contract before she was able to umpire her first game.

The league picked the wrong woman to mess with. Gera took her fight to the New York State Human Rights Commission, protesting that her civil rights had been violated. She won, but the NAPBL made no attempt to reinstate her — so she sued. Magically, within a year, she was given back her umpire's contract.

While umpiring her first professional game, on June 24, 1972, Gera reversed a decision on a call and the rest of the umpiring team was quick to jump on her mistake. She left the field in tears, abandoning her professional career.

once said: "Best thing wrong with Jack Fisher is nothing." (See also Batting Average.)

STRETCH: OK. If you're with me this far, you're ready for the stretch. If you ask four baseball fans what the stretch is, you'll get four different answers. And they'll probably all be wrong. The stretch is a pitching technique. It was developed as a way of pitching the ball very quickly when there are runners on base. In the stretch, the pitcher does not bring the ball over his head or go through a full windup. You see, once the pitcher indicates that he is going to throw the ball to the plate, he can't change his mind and throw to the base. That would be a balk. So once he's begun his pitch, the runner can steal at will. If the pitcher is going through a full windup, his hands come to a set position over his head, then down to his belt again before he stretches back to sling the ball at the plate. With all this going on, even the slowest runner would be halfway to second base before the catcher even gets the ball. So that's where the stretch comes in. With runners on base, the pitcher wants the catcher to get the ball as soon as possible, so he only uses the part of the pitching motion that is absolutely necessary: the stretch.

STRIKE: The first commandment of baseball says: "If thou hast three strikes, thou art out!" But like all commandments, read the fine print. A strike is called when (a) the pitch passes through the strike zone and the batter does not swing; (b) the batter swings at a pitch and misses; or (c) the batter hits the ball into foul territory and nobody catches it. And this is the exception to the rule: The batter can hit as many foul balls as he likes; after two

DID YOU KNOW

That baseball uniforms have always been kitsch? In 1849, the New York Knickerbockers came out with the first official uniform. They wore blue wool pantaloons, white flannel shirts, and straw hats. Cute.

strikes, they stop counting (unless they are caught). A strike is also what nearly killed baseball in 1995.

STRIKE ZONE: Like its cousin, the twilight zone, the strike zone is a mysterious and ever-changing dimension. A rule of thumb is that the strike zone includes all the parts of the male anatomy your mother warned you about; that is, everything between the shoulders and the knees.

STRIKEOUT: When you see a grown man slouch to the dugout with his tail between his legs, you can bet he has struck out. A strikeout can happen in several ways: (a) three pitches through the strike zone; (b) three pitches swung at and missed; (c) any combination of (a) and (b); or (d) a foul bunt with two strikes. Got that? Now get this: If the third strike gets away from the catcher, and the batter can beat the throw to first, he both strikes out and arrives safely at first base. Just like in life, this is very rare, when you can strike out and still get to first base.

SUBMARINE: Have you ever been suckered into watching submarine races? They usually take place just out of eyeshot of "Lovers' Lane." A submarine pitcher is worth watching, though. While most pitchers throw the ball from over their shoulder, a submarine hurler sweeps the ball *under* his shoulder and lets it go from somewhere below. It is very hard for the batter to see what's coming at him from belt level, giving the pitcher the advantage of surprise. It takes cool concentration and a periscope to consistently hit a submarine pitcher.

SUICIDE SQUEEZE PLAY: This is a move of

DID YOU KNOW ?

That baseball fans weren't always called fans? They used to be called kranks.

daring and desperation. You probably know some loser who tries this kind of stuff on women. The runner on third base breaks for home and doesn't care what the batter does. In the squeeze play, the idea is for the batter to bunt the ball. In the suicide version of the play, the runner doesn't wait to see what the batter does, he just hits the dirt and takes his chances. If the batter doesn't manage to hit the ball, the runner is a dead duck.

Pitcher Pat Hentgen, making a point.

SWEEP: Here we go again with the housework. A sweep is when your team wins all the games in a series. Imagine what they could do with a vacuum cleaner!

SWITCH-HITTER: A batter who goes both ways. Now, going both ways has nothing to do with the player's sexual preferences, but it has everything to do with who's pitching. For example, a natural left-handed hitter might "turn the other cheek" — or switch sides — to face a left-handed pitcher, thus eliminating the fundamental advantage the lefty has over left-handed batters.

TAG: Tags are important. If your jeans don't have the right tags, it doesn't matter how you fill them out — those bargain store brand denims just won't make an impression at the park. On the diamond, it doesn't matter what they're wearing; if a player touches a runner with the ball, he's out.

TAG UP: Julia does this to save money. She looks good in anything. She buys bargain store brand

DID YOU KNOW?

That it took a Harvard graduate to invent the catcher's mask? Fred Thayer invented the mask to protect his million dollar smile. That was in 1875. It took hockey another 75 years before their goalies figured out how to keep their teeth.

jeans and sews brand-name tags on the back. As if anybody important is looking at the tags back there. In baseball, tagging up is what the runner had better do on a long fly ball. While the ball is in the air, the runner touches the base he was on prior to the ball being hit. The runner must wait until the ball is caught before leaving the base and running home or to the next base. (See also Sacrifice.)

TAKE: You'd think it has something to do with stealing, wouldn't you? Well it does, but not the way you think. The take signal is a message from the manager: It means you shouldn't swing at the ball no matter what. Maybe the manager has also signaled the runner to steal the next base. The batter doesn't know why he's been given a take sign, and he doesn't ask. He just stands there and lets the ball go by. (See also Red Light.)

TEXAS LEAGUER: A Texas leaguer isn't a guy who plays in a ten-gallon hat. It's a ball that is hit into the shallow part of the outfield. This is the way they do it in Texas? I would have thought they'd hit home runs out on the range.

THOMAS, FRANK: Frank Thomas, "The Big Hurt," is that gigantic first baseman who comes to town with the Chicago White Sox with a slugging percentage nearly triple his weight. If you don't happen to live in Chicago, you understand why they call him "The Big Hurt." The White Sox come to town for a weekend and your best three pitchers

Frank Thomas "The Big Hurt." Can you think of another name for him?

Diamonds are a girls BEST FRIEND

Margaret Gisolo

Margaret Gisolo grew up in a time when playing baseball was as American as voting for the president. She should have known that real baseball, like most other real opportunities, were reserved for the male of the species. When the American Legion organized a national program for young players, they described the program as '...a means of teaching practical Americanism to the youth of the country..." Realizing the importance of Junior Baseball to their continued financial success, the American and National Leagues jumped on the bandwagon, offering financial support to the fledgling operation. Margaret Gisolo tried out for and won a spot on her local team, the Cubs, and was immediately recognized as the team's best player. It didn't take long for the protests to bubble to the surface. Gisolo and the Cubs played a best of three series against a local team, the Clinton Baptists, and Gisolo drove in the winning run in game three. The fat was on the fire. The Clinton team protested that under the American Legion rules, 'any boy was eligible to play...'" and Gisolo wasn't exactly 'any boy'. The controversy over girls in Junior League baseball was argued back and forth, until, at the end of the Cubs winning 1928 season, the American Legion came up with the rule which would stand until the 1970's: No Girls Allowed.

end up in psychoanalysis. I mean, get a grip fellas, it's only a game.

TIME: You've heard that time is relative, haven't you? It's sure true in baseball. In fact, in baseball, it hardly matters at all! It doesn't matter how much of it is required to complete a game. But time is very important. Players call for it whenever they see it as an advantage. It's not that they get a coffee break when they call for time, but they get a break in the action. They hold up a finger or hand and wait for the umpire to call "Time!" or "Time-out!" Next time some chump is too quick for you, hold up a finger and see if anybody tells him to cool his jets.

TOOLS OF IGNORANCE: This is one of the great misnomers of baseball. The catcher, the one player who has to know everything that's going on at every moment, wears the tools of ignorance.

TRADE DEADLINE: When my friend Julia goes to a party, her trade deadline is about 12:30 A.M. If the guy she's been flirting with starts telling horror stories about this three ex-wives, or about how his regular squeeze doesn't understand him, she figures it's about time for a powder-room promenade. If she doesn't dump the deadbeat before the deadline, it'll be too late to scout out a new suitor. In baseball, it means about the same thing. If your team is gonna make a run for the pennant, and they need a guy or two to fill out a weak spot in the lineup, they'd better get their ducks in a row before the trade deadline.

TRIP TO THE MOUND: Every pitcher is allowed one free visit from the bench per inning. The second one costs him the ball. Sounds a bit drastic doesn't it? The trip to the mound is usually taken by the manager or the pitching coach. I've never seen one trip, though. They wear spikes just in case. I mean, why is the guy wearing spikes? He spends the whole night sitting in the dugout spitting! The trip or visit to the mound is sometimes made to talk to the pitcher about what the manager wants to do, but sometimes it's used to buy time for a pitcher warming up in the bull pen. If they come out a second time in the same inning, it's to turn the ball over to another arm.

If this is Thomas's trip to the mound, the pitcher better have life insurance.

TURN TWO: My friend Julia says she can always do this if the guy has enough stamina. (See Double Play.)

TURNER, TED: This is the guy who always brings his team to the World Series and usually goes home without the trophy. You can see Ted with his wife, Jane Fonda, cheering and weeping every October when the Atlanta

DID YOU KNOW

That the first book of baseball lingo was published in the 1880s? The Krank: his language and what it means was written by Thomas Lawson.

Braves come "that close" to winning it all. It's all show biz, though, isn't it? Look for a new Atlanta stadium named after Turner. You can watch it all on CNN. He's in charge of that too.

TWO-WAY CONTRACT: It's like a Vegas wedding. If it works out, great; you may have many happy years ahead of you. On the other hand, if you go into a slump, or if your phenom turns out to be an early bloomer, it's easy to send him packing. A ball player with a two-way contract is a minor-leaguer who can be called up to the big team any time they need him. (See also Cup of Coffee.)

UMPIRE: We think of the umpire as the fat, uptight guy behind the catcher who looks for all the world like a chronic PMS sufferer. That's true, as far as it goes. In fact, there are a whole entourage of people who judge the game. There is the guy behind the plate, a guy at first, one at second, and one at third. In the World Series, there are two more added along the foul lines. If only you had these guys at the dinner table to settle family squabbles.

UNEARNED RUN: So who cares whether it's earned or not, it *counts* doesn't it? The only one to care about whether a run is earned or not is the pitcher. If the runner gets on base when he shouldn't be there, say he gets to base on an error, then if he scores, it is an unearned run and has no effect on the pitcher's ERA.

VAUGHN, MO: I looked up Mo Vaughn in the Who's Who in Baseball, and it said he weighed 225 pounds. I've been known to lie about my

Diamonds are a girls BEST FRIEND

THE GIRL WHO STRUCK OUT RUTH AND GERHIG

You may have heard of Jackie Mitchell. Baseball's gender barrier is solid, but this kid slipped through a hole and into the headlines. She first signed a minor league contract in 1931, and baseball took notice. They called her the first woman to play in professional baseball. Of course, it wasn't true, Lizzie Arlington had already done that, but the headlines crowed about the Chattanooga Lookouts and their stand out southpaw, Jackie Mitchell. It wasn't long before the rookie's talents would be put to the ultimate test. An April exhibition game had been scheduled between the Lookouts and the New York Yankees. The papers responded in spades, with reporters and film crews traveling from across the country to cover this unlikely event: the greatest hitting team in history would face a 17 year old girl. Babe Ruth was the third batter in the lineup: The Lookouts brought in Jackie Mitchell. The Sultan of Swat struck out in four. Exactly what smiling Lou Gerhig said to Ruth on his way to the plate we don't know, but we know that Gehrig swung at three and followed the worlds greatest hitter into the dugout. Was it a gimmick, or did she really strike out the two best hitters in the game? Could she do it again? We'll never know. The next morning, the Commissioner of Baseball voided Mitchell's contract, on the inexplicable grounds that the game was "too strenuous" for a woman.

Mo Vaughn says he weights 225 pounds. So, who's gonna argue?

weight, too, but I've never shaved 40 pounds off the truth! If you sit in the front rows when Boston comes to town, you can feel the ground shake when this big galoot comes to the plate. One of his teammates, who preferred to remain anonymous, said: "Mo looks fat and slow, but I'd never say that to his face"

VISITORS: These visitors are not like your cousin Sally, her hungry husband, three kids, and Irish Wolfhound who come in from Cleveland for a short visit in July and don't leave until their mail has started arriving in August. Welcomed visiting teams come to town, stay two or three days, and then move along. Baseball is so polite: They let the visitors bat first.

WADDELL, RUBE: You've heard that there's one born every minute, haven't you? In the baseball books, there are 30 of them listed — Rubes, that is. The strangest of them was Rube Waddell. Waddell would sometimes hold up a game because he was busy playing marbles with the local kids outside the stadium. It was written into his contract that he would not eat animal crackers in bed. In exhibition games, he would often tell all the fielders to sit down while he struck out the side. But he wasn't just weird, he was good! In his long career, he pitched 50 shutouts and struck out three times as many batters as he walked.

WAGNER, HONUS: Wagner played at the same time as Ty Cobb, and except for being every bit as good a player, he was Cobb's opposite. Wagner was the model of a gentleman: polite, fair-minded, and intelligent. Cobb was none of these things and got

DID YOU KNOW

That the first body-hugging uniform came into vogue in 1888? The New York Giants decided that every day should be Ladies Day and appeared sporting tight black pants and matching shirts. The men called them "funeral uniforms"; the women called them "flattering." I call it progress.

all the headlines. This giant of the game was with the Pittsburgh organization for 56 years — 17 as a player and 39 as the manager. Although he is still regarded as one of the greatest players to ever pull on a uniform, he is best remembered for his 1909 baseball card, "The Wagner," which is worth half a million dollars.

WAIVERS: Just like the autograph seekers hanging around the stadium waving pencils and programs, players try to get past them unless they're being offered something they like. Waivers is a complicated procedure under which any team can buy up the remainder of a player's contract for a bargain basement price. If a player is being dropped from a roster and all the other teams give him a waiver, he says *Adios* and becomes a free agent. After waivers he can sign a new contract with any team that comes up with enough dough. (See also Free Agent; Reserve Clause.)

WALK: Any player who has four balls does not have to *run* to first base. He walks. It's not that they figure he's got enough to contend with, it means that the pitcher was not able to fool him into swinging at three unhittable pitches. There are several ways to get four balls. There's the normal way (see Base on Balls), there's the deliberate walk (see Free Pass), and there's a little known situation which is known only to more advanced students of the game: If the pitcher balks with three balls and no runners on base, then the balk is called ball four, and the runner scampers up the line. This is very unusual and includes the following pitching offenses: (1) a double pump; (2) a quick pitch; (3) any other illegal pitch; or (4) the pitcher brings his

---

DID YOU KNOW ?

That the first "rain check" was issued in Detroit in 1888? Holders of tickets for a rained out game were admitted free of charge for the next scheduled match.

throwing hand to his mouth before pitching the ball. In these cases (a balk with no runners on base), the balk is called ball four and the batter goes to first base on balls. (See also Balk.)

WALKER, LARRY: This Canadian kid wanted to be a National Hockey League goalie, and it was a good thing for baseball that he wasn't good enough! He always wanted to play in Montreal, but he expected to be playing for the Canadiens, not the Expos. Currently working in that other great hockey town, Denver, Walker is best known for his incredibly accurate and powerful arm. The "Canuck Kid" has been known to throw runners out at first base. From right field!

WARNING TRACK: Like that built-in alarm that goes off when you take that first bite of a chocolate eclair, the warning track tells the outfielder he'd better watch out. The warning track is an area between the outfield grass and the home run fence whose rough texture tells the back-pedaling fielder that the fence is right behind him.

Juan Gonzales in full swing. This young slugger rarley chooses to walk.

Diamonds are a girls BEST FRIEND

BABE DIDRIKSON

Babe Didrikson was an all star in all sports, a double Olympic Gold medalist in track, and her own biggest fan. The only thing she never won in sports was a Big League baseball contract. They called her 'Babe', not on account of her good looks, but on account of her powerful swing. Following her performance at the 1932 Los Angeles Olympics, where she won two gold medals and one silver, she played one brief season with the only baseball organization of her time who would take the chance on a female pitcher, the House of David. With the barnstorming Davids, she played exhibition games against minor and major league teams, and for the first time in her life, she was humbled. She played well enough against the minor leaguers, but when Major League batters stepped in, she was no match for their experience and power. Some people still argue that Didrikson was never cut out to be a pitcher, and could have fielded and run bases as well as any professional ball player of her time, but the question remains academic. In the 1930's, just like today, women are not welcome on professional baseball diamonds. So she took her powerful swing to another sport, and dominated women's professional golf until her death in 1956.

WEBSTER, DANIEL: This isn't the guy who wrote the dictionary. That's Noah Webster. Daniel Webster was an orator — a polite way of saying the guy couldn't stop once his mouth got into gear. They call a manager who can't stay off the field Daniel Webster, but they also call the batter, catcher, first baseman, or umpire Daniel Webster if they mutter, gab, or swear when they should shut up and play ball.

WETTELAND, JOHN: John Wetteland throws so much gas, he ought to work in a filling station. His fuel-injected fastball comes across the plate at 98 miles an hour. His opponents complain about his nasty split-finger pitch that nobody can hit, but his teammates complain about his hat. The sweat-stained cap that he hasn't washed since 1990 has a locker all of its own because nobody wants to share a room with it. Wetteland has worked around the National League for years but is currently assigned to the New York night shift, as the closer for the American League's Yankees.

WHIFF: Whether you are in the locker room or at the plate, a whiff is something you want to avoid. The inning is late, the batter's side is down, and the tying run is at third. The batter feels he's gonna hit that ball come hell or high water. The pitch comes in low and inside and the bat comes around like a dervish on Benzedrine: plenty of power, but a little too high. If you've ever been near enough to the plate to hear Tony Fernandez say his prayers, you've probably heard the likes of Jose Canseco or Fred McGriff "whiff" one. It's named after the sound of a bat meeting fresh air: whiff.

❓ DID YOU KNOW

That in 1979 two brothers faced each other as starting pitchers? On May 31, 1979, Tom Underwood started for the Tigers while his brother Pat, in his major-league debut, started for the Toronto Blue Jays. But the Underwood brothers were not the first to do this: In 1927, Jesse (Dodgers) and Virgil (Giants) Barnes were the starting pitchers for this classic crosstown match-up.

WILLIAMS, TED: You have to know who Ted Williams was because every time somebody hits over .360, they start calling him "The Next Ted Williams." Ted Williams was the last player to average a hit four out of every 10 times at bat. He hit .406 in 1941, and nobody has ever come close since. (See also Batting Average.)

WINNING PITCHER: You might say a winning pitcher is anybody who can get millions of dollars to play 35 or 40 ball games. But it's not as simple as that. The starting pitcher, if he is to be the winning pitcher, has to toss at least five innings and has to be ahead when he leaves the game. If his team is ahead when he leaves, but goes behind at any point after that, then even if the team wins the game, he's not the winning pitcher. Got that? Now, if a reliever takes over when the team is behind and is in the game when the team goes ahead, he will be the winning pitcher, if the team wins the game.

WORLD SERIES: OK, it isn't that the whole world has a chance to play, it's only each championship team from the National League and the

DID YOU KNOW?

That the first president of the United States to watch a game while in office was Benjamin Harrison? His visit to the park was on June 2, 1892.

American League. Since 1903, the two league championship teams have met in October to see who has the best team. In 1904, to satisfy a cranky Boston manager, they introduced special rules for playing the World Series. The rules are hardly different from the normal ones, but they satisfied the curmudgeon. (See also Brush Rules.)

One-armed pitcher Jim Abbot gives new meaning to the term "Lefty."

DID YOU KNOW?

That Babe Ruth hit his first professional home run in Toronto? If you are a Canadian, you might have known but you probably didn't know that his Canadian homer was the only one he hit in his minor-league career. If you are a resident of Fayetteville, North Carolina, then you probably think he hit his first pro home run there, but that was an exhibition game.

YOGI BERRAISMS: Baseball is a thinking person's game, but it is not exactly known for philosophical sophistication. But there is an exception to this general rule: The game's number one ranked philosopher was a catcher named Yogi Berra. The man who said "How can you think and hit at the same time?" was definitely smarter than the average bear. So insightful were his comments on the game that they have become an integral part of the baseball language. He gave us the first rule of baseball: "It ain't over till it's over." And the second: "In baseball, you don't know nothing." He had a remarkable optimism, for a streaky hitter: "Slump? I ain't in no slump. I just ain't hitting." And his general philosophy is a lesson to us all: "You can observe a lot by watching." And finally, Yogi gave us advice that could keep you awake at night, pondering: "When you come to a fork in the road, take it."

ZEILE, TODD: This standout third baseman is a dead ringer for Tom Berringer, and though Zeile never did a smokin' hot scene with Mimi Rogers, he did have 100 RBIs for St. Louis in 1993. Look for zealot Todd Zeile at the hot corner with Baltimore these days.

Ladies DAY

SELECTED BIBLIOGRAPHY

Alvarez, Mark. *The Official Baseball Hall Of Fame Answer Book.* New York: Simon & Schuster, 1989.

Angell, Roger. *The Summer Game.* New York: Viking Press, 1972.

Appel, Martin. *Baseball's Best: The Hall Of Fame Gallery.* McGraw Hill, 1977.

Appel, Martin. *The First Book Of Baseball.* New York: Crown, 1988.

Astor, Gerald. *The Baseball Hall of Fame 50th Anniversary Book.* New York: Prentice Hall Press, 1988.

Aylesworth, Thomas G. *The Kids' World Almanac Of Baseball.* New York: World Almanac, 1990.

Benagh, Jim. *Baseball: Startling Stories Behind The Records.* New York: Sterling, 1987.

Benson, Michael. *Ballparks of North America: A Comprehensive Historical Reference To Baseball Grounds, Yards and Stadiums.* Jefferson, N.C.: McFarland, 1989.

Berler, Ron. *The Super Book Of Baseball.* Boston: Little, Brown, 1991.

Blake, Mike. *The Incomplete Book of Baseball Superstitions, Rituals and Oddities.* New York: Wynwood Press, 1991.

Cataneo, David. *Peanuts And Crackerjack: A Treasury Of Baseball Legends And Lore.* San Diego: Harcourt Brace, 1991.

Clary, Jack T. *So You Think You're A Baseball Fan: What Every Knowable Baseball Fan Should Know.* Boston: Quinlan Press, 1988.

Dewey, Donald. *The Biographical History Of Baseball.* New York: Carroll & Graf, 1995.

Dreayer, Barry. *Baseball.* Los Angeles: General Publishing Group, 1994.

Einstein, Charles. *The Baseball Reader: Favorites From The Fireside Books Of Baseball.* New York: McGraw-Hill, 1980.

Fiffer, Steve. *How To Watch Baseball: A Fan's Guide To Savoring The Fine Points Of The Game.* Facts On File. 1987.

Forker, Dom. *Almost Everything You've Ever Wanted To Know About Baseball.* Toronto: Parurian Press, 1978.

Forker, Dom. *Baseball Brain Teasers: Major League Puzzlers.* New York: Sterling, 1986.

Garber, Angus G. *Inside Baseball: Teams, Traditions And Players.* New York: Friedman/Fairfax, 1994.

Gregorich, Barbara. *Women At Play.* A Harvest Original, Harcourt Brace & Company, 1993.

Gutman, Dan. *The Way Baseball Works.* New York: Simon & Schuster, 1996.

Hollander, Zander. *The Baseball Book.* New York: Random House, 1991.

Hoppel, Joe. *The Sporting News Baseball Trivia 2.* St. Louis, Mo.; Sporting News Pub. Co., 1987.

Jacobs G., and J. R. McCroy. *Baseball Rules In Pictures.* New York: Putnam, 1985.

Jordan, Godfrey. *The Official Kids' Book of Baseball.* Toronto: Random House Of Canada, 1993.

Kahn, Roger. *The Boys Of Summer.* New York: Harper & Row, 1972.

Koppet, Leonard. *The New Thinking Fan's Guide To Baseball.* New York: Simon & Schuster, 1991.

Leitner, Irving. *Baseball: Diamonds In The Rough.* New York: Abeland-Schuman, 1972.

McFarlane, Brian. *It Happened In Baseball: Amazing Tales From The Fields Of Dreams.* Toronto: Stoddart, 1993.

Nabhan, Marty. *Cy Young Winners.* Vero. Beach, Fla.: Rourke Corp., 1991.

Okrent, Daniel. *Baseball Anecdotes.* New York: Harper & Row, 1989.

Okrent, Daniel. *Nine Innings.* New York: Ticknor & Fields, 1985.

Peterson, Harold. *The Man Who Invented Baseball.* New York: Scribner, 1973.

Salisbury, Luke. *The Answer Is Baseball.* New York: Vintage Books/Random House, 1989.

Schoor, Gene. *The History of the World Series: The Complete Chronology Of America's Greatest Sports Tradition.* New York: William Morrow Co., 1990.

Shatzkin, Mike. *The Ballplayers: Baseballs Ultimate Biographical Reference.* New York: Arbor House/William Morrow, 1990.

Thorn, John. *The Armchair Book Of Baseball.* New York: Scribner's, 1985.

Walker, Henry. *Illustrated Baseball Dictionary For Young People.* New York: Harvey House, 1970.

Ward, Geoffrey C., and Ken Burns. *Baseball An Illustrated History.* New York: Alfred A. Knopf, 1994.

Ward, Geoffrey C., and Ken Burns, with S. A. Kramer. *Baseball 25 Great Moments.* New York: Alfred A. Knopf, 1994.